BEHIND
THE MADNESS

SAMUEL COLE

ISBN 979-8-89243-551-2 (paperback)
ISBN 979-8-89243-552-9 (digital)

Christian Faith Publishing
832 Park Avenue
Meadville, PA 16335
www.christianfaithpublishing.com

Printed in the United States of America

Contents

CHAPTER 1

Busted

I've noticed whenever life gets a little too comfortable, there always seems to be an external force that sends me down a dark rabbit hole without a bottom. Sometimes the story gets so dark that it seems to become entangled inside the web that makes me, me. That's when I know that I will never be the same again.

Well, this is one of those stories. Personally, it scares the hell out of me, and I'm sure it's going to scare a lot of other people too. I'm not a writer by profession or a linguistic expert by far. To this day I'm debating back and forth whether to release this story or not. It has to do with the Ferguson effect riots back in the day and how everything that we're going through now all started back then. Anonymity is nice, but if I say nothing the rest of my life, that wouldn't be right either.

The year was 2013 and in the middle of November. I was living in a large two-story house with an attached garage. It had a nice yard with a barn in the back where I set up an art studio. The house was almost paid off with a few more payments to go. I was living with my best friend Tammy, her two sons, and our nine-month-old baby girl, Olivia. Life was good. I was working hard, making ends meet as a remodeling contractor doing basement and office remodels for a company that appreciated my performance and my ability to get the job done under budget. Tammy worked as an OB medical nurse at a local hospital delivering babies. With both of us working, it was nice to have two grown boys at the house to fill in watching Olivia when Tammy and I weren't home.

I was driving home from a bar after work one day when I noticed a cop car kitty-corner from the street I was turning down. That's when I made that right on this road called Heart. I was thinking to myself, *I'm not speeding, but did I use my turn signal? Just don't look up, Sam.* I didn't get my license back after my last DUI, and it just so happened I was driving home from a bar knowing I was going to blow numbers. There was no way I was going to go through this DUI crap all over again.

When I looked up into my rearview mirror, that's when I see the lights—the blue and red flashing lights that were reflecting off the snow in the night sky. I was just out of the police officer's sight, driving down this hill. I didn't want to take a chance, so I stepped on it and took a left into a subdivision, the first one I came across. Then I pulled into a stranger's driveway as quickly as I could and waited.

I'd pulled this maneuver before, and it worked. She probably would have never seen me if I hadn't forgotten to turn off my headlights. My car being the only light to be seen down in this little subdivision, I knew I was in trouble.

After the cop passed up the road I was on, I was thinking if she had seen me or not. Well, maybe she didn't. Or did she? When she turned around, she passed the road again and spotted my car, then did a quick U-turn and turned onto the street that I was on. She rolled down the street real slow. When she pulled up to my car, she put her spotlight on. With her bright blue and red lights flashing, she got out of her squad car and walked up to my window. It seemed like it took forever for the whole event to take place.

When she got to my window, she shone her flashlight into my eyes and asked, "Do you live here, sir?"

I said, "No, ma'am."

Then some guy with a confused look on his face came out of the house of the driveway I was in. When she noticed him, she said, "Step out of the car, sir."

"Okay, this is going to suck," I said to myself. I slowly stepped out of this piece of crap car I was in.

"Do you have a license, sir?" she asked.

"Um, no, ma'am," I said.

She asked me some more questions. "Have you been drinking tonight, sir?"

"No, ma'am."

"If you don't mind, we'll do a field sobriety or a breathalyzer."

"I'm going to have to refuse to do that, ma'am," I said as politely as I could. I could tell she was getting frustrated now with her tone of voice. She handcuffed me, read me my rights, and put me in the back of her squad car. Cops, I'm sure, hate it when you act like this because they need to prove that you've been drinking, and as long as you're not slurring your words or fighting with them, it's hard to get a DUI to stick.

So I got arrested, and they ended up bringing me in for suspicion of drinking and driving and driving without a license. When she took me to their local police station, she made me sit for a couple of hours in a holding cell. I'd been through all this before. Cops always like to do this and try to trick you by saying, "See, you've been sitting for a couple of hours. Why don't you blow and do our sobriety test so you can prove yourself innocent?" Then they follow up with the questions. But I knew better. I knew that all it would take was for me to have the smallest amount of alcohol on my breath or maybe if I slurred my words when she was questioning me, and I would be done for sure. I knew about all the little cameras they had in there. I was trying my hardest to get out of this one. It was hard not to get angry in there, so I did my best to keep as quiet as I could because everyone knows as soon as you get pulled over for a DUI, your life is going to change for the worse for a very, very long time.

As I was sitting here as quietly as I could, I began to think. When are those autonomous vehicles coming out? I guess if you were blacked out drunk and gotten into an accident or something. Is it really the MADD (mothers against drinking and driving), or is there an ulterior motive for these people? Why not give people BAIID systems in people's cars after they get arrested for a DUI instead of taking away a person's freedom? Just have people who get caught blow into those little machines before they can start their cars. The

Secretary of the State finally ends up giving you one, but it's not until you attend all the Alcoholics Anonymous (AA) programs with no way to get back and forth. Then there's the money you have to spend on the schooling and the fines, which could end up being more than ten thousand dollars. After that comes the money you have to spend on the special lawyer to go downtown to attend a special hearing. It's just an endless number of hoops that they make you jump through first. They're doing it for the money, not necessarily out of the safety of the drivers in my opinion.

It gets people mad enough to give up and just drive without one. Which happened in my case. It's an endless spinning hamster wheel that they put you on. Data have shown that being angry while speeding and using cell phones are the leading cause of death over drinking and driving by a lot. With a bar within a mile or two in any given direction, these cops are shooting fish in a barrel.

I was looking at some serious prison time considering my license was still revoked from my last DUI. With it being my third one, I was looking to go to prison for the next two to three years. With a baby at the house, I wanted to make it as hard as possible for these people to throw me away. Prosecuting attorneys are looking to keep their jobs just like everyone else is. There is no way they're going to take someone to trail unless they know that they can win.

Calm down, Sam. Don't lose it here. No matter what you do. I was just sitting in their police station with all these thoughts in my head, trying to shut them off. Just trying to keep my mouth shut in there was difficult, but I was doing it. I was stuck in their office with cameras all over me, I'm sure, with some prosecuting attorney watching every move I made. So I tried not to react the best I could as I sat there with their threatening comments on how they were going to take away my freedom and everything I cared about away from me if I didn't cooperate and do their little sobriety tests. Then she said to me, "If you have nothing to hide, well then, you would be cooperating with us now, wouldn't you?"

I said, "No, ma'am, I've been through this before and sorry to say I don't trust you."

I just kept telling myself what my lawyer said from my last DUI. Keep your mouth shut. I kept his words in the back of my head. He said to me, "Rule number one: Never blow. Just refuse all the tests that try to make you do. Rule number two: Keep your mouth shut and call me. If I don't answer right away, don't worry. I check my phone every morning. I'll get to you as soon as I can. Rule number three: Trust the system. Let the courts handle it."

I knew that I was in trouble this time with a newborn baby at the house and me just having paid off my lawyer from my last DUI. I knew I wasn't going to be able to afford to pay off any kind of fancy lawyer this time. I knew whatever bond they were going to set for was going to be too high considering I only had about $800 to my name.

I refused to do any of their tests, and I just kept as quiet as I could. I didn't get into an accident. I forgot to turn on my turn signal. How much trouble could I be in? I could hear the prosecuting attorney on the speaker phone as he was talking to one of the arresting officers. "Yep, bring him in. He didn't pay off his fine of $5,000 dollars from his last DUI. I have a warrant for his arrest."

I thought I had more time to pay that off. *Okay, I'm done for*, I thought to myself. I swear they got this whole system rigged. Calm down, Sam. You're cool, don't freak out. Everything will be fine. You're cool. They have nothing on you. Hopefully, you won't serve too much time this time.

After they handcuffed me, they led me outside to the back of one of their squad cars. It was a lot smaller back there than it looked. What with me being six foot four, 240 pounds, there wasn't much room for me or anyone who stands over five feet tall to sit comfortably in there. So here I was, curled up into a ball position the whole way to the county jail, which was a half hour away.

When I finally got there, they helped me get out of their squad car by dragging me out, what with it being the only way I could have fulfilled their request of getting out of that sardine can. When I stood up, they took off the cuffs that were a quarter inch imbedded in my wrists. That's when I saw bruising already starting to form. As soon as they took the cuffs off, I started to massage my wrists to stop them from hurting.

After my courtesy ride to the Lake County Jail, they finger-printed me and put me in a holding cell, which they liked to call the drunk tank. Before one of the guards slammed the door to the cell, he said I must wait here for two days till I could see the judge. Because if you get arrested on a Saturday, the judge doesn't come back to hear your case until the following Monday. I didn't have the five-thousand-dollar bond, so maybe I was hoping for a bond reduction on Monday before I started to ask people for money.

I was not looking forward to talking to Tammy about this. When I called her, I let her know where I was. After about a ten-minute lecture on how "she told me so," we said our goodbyes. Well, at least I did. She hung up before she could say hers.

I was stuck in this little holding cell. I would say it was ten feet by twenty feet. It sounds big until you have eight or so other guys in there with you. They liked to call it the drunk tank because basically that's what it was, but in my eyes, it should have been called the detox room. Everyone in there seemed to be dope sick to the point where there should have been two toilets in that little cell, instead of the one that was in there for all to see.

In the cell there was no bed, just a cold concrete floor to sleep on and this stainless-steel toilet with a connecting sink. There were a few extra toilet paper rolls, so I took one for a makeshift pillow for the first night anyway. I got a little shut-eye from about 11:00 p.m. to 2:00 a.m., which was for about three hours. See, we ran out of toilet paper when one of the guys was detoxing, and he was making a mess everywhere. Damn, the exhaust fans suck in there. After getting over the smell, I tried like hell just to keep warm in that place and get whatever sleep I could.

When I first walked into this cell, I noticed everyone was putting their head in their shirts. I wondered, What the heck are these guys doing? All of them with their hands in their armpits and their heads in their neck collars as they breathed heavily. I found myself doing the same thing ten minutes later, freezing, with my teeth chattering, trying to get some sleep. We would all try to ask for a pillow or blanket, but anything we would try to ask for just fell on deaf ears. They said their reason not to give us one was that you could use anything that they gave you as a weapon to harm yourself or someone else. Until you were processed and seen by a psychologist, they didn't want to give you anything, not even a pillow. But in my opinion, they wanted to make it as uncomfortable as possible so you would make bail so they would get paid, or also, maybe then they wouldn't have to deal with you.

After having barely any sleep for the last two nights, Monday came, and it was time to take my picture. They don't take your picture right away when you first come in, because the worst off you look in a picture they take of you, the guiltier you look in my opinion. That picture follows you wherever you go until your case is over. With my hair in a mess, my eyes half open and this crooked smile on my face from the lack of sleep, they took my picture.

After they took my picture, they put me in front of the judge. The judge looked at me, then the picture. He just shook his head reading my driving record. Then the judge said I would have to wait here for about a month till my next court date unless I could afford bond and bond out with the five-thousand-dollar bail he set it for. It was way too much money for me to come up with. *Well, looks like I'll be here awhile*, I thought. *Luckily, I have a wife who works.* After getting done paying off the house, the only big bills we were paying for were our hospital bills from our daughter Olivia when she was born.

Well, maybe I could get some sober time and reflect on becoming a better man and father when I got out. It's not like I wasn't one before—changing diapers, working all the time to help support my family. But spending any amount of money purely for my own personal enjoyment without even a college fund and, on top of that, taking risks like driving home from a bar after work—there was room for improvement. The main reason I spent money was to relieve stress from working so much. But it seemed to have worked for me. Stress is a killer. In some cases, it will kill you faster than the bottle can. It's so much easier to be happy drinking than to be pissed off sober.

I was thinking back to the other day. I was reading the newspaper about this girl whom I used to date back in high school who got thirteen years in prison for improper lane usage while she was drinking and driving. I was wondering if I was going to get that same treatment. The paragraph in the newspaper went on to say that she could have gotten as much as thirty years. No accident, no harm done to anyone else. No malicious intent. Just getting behind the wheel after a night of drinking with the girls. Now she was on probation for her fifth while she got her sixth. Still, how can violent offenders get a five-year prison sentence and a simple driving offense hold a ten-year prison sentence? Second-degree murder charges hold a lesser prison sentence.

I could see that she needed to be punished. But to send that poor girl to prison for over a decade to prove a point that drinking and driving is bad…I was just thinking of her kids and what kind of anger and resentment they will hold against authority and police in general in the future. Poor girl. I felt sorry for her.

After being stuck in this cell for a couple of days, I was finally getting out of the drunk tank. The other guys were jealous, yelling, "When is it going to be my turn?" "Where's my phone call?" These guys smelled bad after not showering for a couple days. I guess we all did. That's when I took a whiff of my armpit, and it made me a little woozy over the smell after being in there for so long. That smell was coming from me. *Who I am to judge?* I thought. The smell of vomit was thick when I stood up as well. When I looked down at my pants, I noticed there was a dark-pink stain on my thigh. When I looked back in the cell, there was a pool of vomit where I had just got up from and a guy who was passed out on the floor next to it. "Gross," I said, shaking off the chunks off my pants as I followed one of the guards into the changing room where they had me take a shower. He said to me before he closed the door, "Looks like you had some fun in there" as he pointed to the stain on my pants. "Funny," I found myself saying, what with it being my only response.

After my shower, I followed the guard with the five other guys who had court that day to the elevators. They finally moved me to a cell on the second floor of the facility where they gave me a few pairs of scrubs, three pairs of underwear, three pairs of socks, and a few T shirts. The guards made me put all my clothing, toothbrush, and a cup in this long tube sheet that would later act as my sheet for my bed later.

When I got changed and had everything that they gave me packed, the guard made me walk over the elevator doors where I was sent up to the third floor. Now the third floor is the place where classification puts all the newcomers into where they determine your risk factor. Classification wants to make sure you don't belong to any gangs, and if you were, then they would make sure that you wouldn't be housed with someone in a rival gang.

The guard put me in cell five of this two-floor wing that had forty or so cells in it. I just always remember being so cold in there as well. I always would be coming up with new ways to stick something over the vent, with it continuously blowing cold air out. Maybe toothpaste, yeah, I would use it like glue and hold a piece of paper over it. With the full blast of air that came out of it, the paper would eventually fall off. Then I would grab toilet paper, wet it, then put toothpaste on it. Then I would turn that into a mold to stick that to the register. That seemed to hold for a few days anyway until that fell off as well.

All the guys seemed nice enough until one of them wanted something from someone. They were mostly all spoiled kids with too much time on their hands. There were some older guys in there too. Funny, the game Candy Land was in there. Picture this: There were these three huge older black guys sitting around the game with all of them standing well over six feet tall, playing the game. They all turned to me as I was walking through the door, with all of them looking at me with the most intimidating look on their faces when I walked in. These guys had tattoos all over their necks, up and down their arms. One man even had one on his face. I just didn't really want to make eye contact with these guys for fear that I might laugh at them.

Well, the guy with the face tattoo stood up, lifted the Candy Land game, and threw it all the way across the room, pieces went flying everywhere, then yelled, "You guys are cheaters." Then he went back to his room where he began to throw his stuff around, throwing a temper tantrum. Funny, three of the biggest badass gangbangers getting into a fight over a kid's game. I was new there, and I found it funny. It was pretty hard not to laugh. I just kept my mouth shut and looked away, hoping they didn't notice me noticing that what I found them doing was amusing. It was just so out of place. I guess they got sick of playing spades or something, which most of the inmates were playing at the time.

These cooks must be putting something in the food to make these guys act this way, I thought. I did hear when you give a man too much soy in their food, their testosterone levels go down, and their estrogen levels go up. They did serve us a limited amount of meat there. And whatever meat that they did serve contained a lot of soy in it. But I wouldn't put it past them to do something like that on purpose to lessen the chance of fighting that went on in that place.

All these inmates seemed to be on some sort of medication. There were forty or so guys, and I would say more than two-thirds of the guys had to wait every morning and evening in a line to see the nurse when she came in. I truly believe with all the lawsuits that were going on in there, they were ready to give these guys whatever they wanted just so they wouldn't lose their jobs. It seemed everyone in there had a lawsuit going on for something.

I got word one of the guys with whom I spent a couple of days in the drunk tank died from alcohol withdrawal. I guess the nurse got in big trouble for that one because I hadn't seen her since. One of the guys in here said to me, "That guy's family is going to get paid."

I said, "Why?"

"If you die in here, the family gets at least a half a million-dollar lawsuit," this guy at my lunch table was telling me.

"That's crazy," I said in disbelief. Keeping these guys quiet and alive seemed to be their biggest concern here. In my head, though, I couldn't help to think on how much of my tax dollars were being wasted on these assholes. Now it seemed as if I was one of them.

It was cutthroat for the guards in there too; it was easy for one to get written up and lose their jobs. This one woman prison guard got smacked in the butt by an inmate while I was in there. But instead of getting mad and reprimanding him for it, she just turned to him and gave him a smile and giggled afterward. It was all caught on camera, and she was let go the next day.

There were a lot of women guards in there where they seemed to be sexually aroused by these inmates. They would do their hair up nicely and put on a lot of makeup. I would see some of them check themselves out in the mirror just before they would step onto the cell block. You could tell in the eyes of some of them that they were enjoying domineering these men.

One of the female officers the year before—I heard—got caught having an affair with one of the inmates. I guess the reason that she got caught was that she was sneaking food from the outside to him. He was eating steaks, lobster tails, candy. She even snuck in food for all his buddies for New Year's the year before. All of them got Subway sandwiches that day. The only reason she got caught is when someone who didn't get one got jealous and told on her. They looked at the recorded surveillance tapes and saw her sneaking him food as well as sneaking him into the bathroom late at night for a quick poke.

There was a big lawsuit for that inmate as well. He said that the woman was blackmailing him for sex. He called it rape saying she forced him to do it, or else he would be thrown into solitary confinement. I found that one hard to believe. But he ended up getting a big money settlement from that one as well. The county also had his charges dropped and was released the next day. It made me mad. Not that I was jealous that he got paid. Well, maybe a little bit. But mostly because it wasn't out of the pocket of that woman security guard. It was out of the pocket of all the Illinois taxpayers. I must pay almost $8,000 a year in property taxes. This gangbanger just got a piece of that from having sex with one security guard. That was one of my sexual fantasies growing up as a kid. I have to admit, I was a little jealous.

This place just wasn't what I expected a jail would be like. I was locked up in a cell alone for two weeks, getting out for only four hours a day for rec (recreation) time, that's if this place wasn't on lockdown, which occurs in here quite often. Every time there was fight or they had to move someone who was dangerous, the whole jail would be on lockdown, where you were not to leave your cells that whole day. Where was my yard time? I was going crazy locked up for most of the day all alone.

When I did get a chance to get out to the rec room, I would be watching TV. It was so loud in this place it felt as if I was in a crowded airport. Guys would be yelling all day at each other over all the chess games and card games that were going on at that time. The phone people were always fighting over who was next on the phone. Trying to hear the TV was nearly impossible.

I did see something on the news about this place. It had channel 7 news crew come in downstairs and interviewed one of the officers about a death that occurred the night before. I guess there was a woman who was dragged to her cell by one of the guards, but unbeknownst to him she had a broken neck, I guess, and she died the next day. It would be hard to tell which people were faking it and which were the ones that were really hurt. But I'm sure he lost his job for that one too. I couldn't tell you for sure because I couldn't hear the TV with all the noise that this pod was making.

After rec time was over, back to the cell alone I went. I mostly spent my time reading and drawing. But every night I would look forward to getting a visit from a mouse, which I named Mr. Gingles like in the movie *The Green Mile*. He was a cute, little furball. I would feed him from time to time. He never went into any other cell than mine. I never knew why. Maybe there was a guy before me who was feeding the little guy too. It did feel good to have company when I was in there even if it was just a mouse. It was so lonely in there, just me and my thoughts. They had us locked away alone in our cells for most of the day.

In the mornings it was always a mad dash to the phone, which I was able to get on surprisingly today. I talked to Tammy whenever I could. I would make her put Olivia on the phone even though she couldn't talk yet. At least Tammy was cool about the situation. We talked a lot over the phone while I was in there. It seemed like she would be gloating a lot as if to say, "See, that's why I had been nagging at you for all those years about your drinking."

After the two weeks I spent in their classification cell, they finally figured I was okay to put in general population, so they took me to cell block 2 where it was more open and cleaner than the last one. Over here there were two-people cells. It gave me a chance to talk to somebody. I spent a long time in that cell alone with someone I had never met before. If you ever go through this experience, it is always better to be on the top bunk 'cause if you get the bottom bunk, your face is going to be about three feet away from someone who was pooping every morning. It is not the most pleasing thing to wake up to.

He was okay, I guess. His name was Kenny. Skinny, tall white kid, about twenty or so, with long black hair. I learned that he worked in construction too. He showed me how to work the commissary machine where you can buy noodles and snacks. It was a machine called a kiosk so that you could see how much money was in your books to make phone calls as well.

My jail number came up as 64216. Kenny and one of the guards who was helping us said to add three more numbers so they could identify me through the machine. It ended in a 6, so I added three more sixes out of convenience. The guard who was helping us said, "Don't do that!"

I said, "Why?"

He said, "Jeez, you know that number is going to follow you to every court proceeding that you have while you're here." It was too late. I already pressed enter. After that, I turned to Kenny, put both of my pointer fingers to my head, and said jokingly, "Hail Satan."

We shared a laugh and went back to playing some more chess together, which is what kept us busy most of the time I was there. I wasn't a bad chess player. I thought I was pretty good until I started playing with some of these guys. Kenny and I were a good matchup, but some of these other guys who were in and out of the system were beating me every game. They would smack the table when they won. There was a lot of rubbing your nose in it when you lost at something in here. I didn't play much chess there after that. It got me mad sometimes, getting beat in chess by people who, on the surface, didn't seem to be that smart. I was impressed. I just didn't like to lose.

We played a lot of spades together there too. I played with my cellie, Kenny, as my partner. We did well for the most part. We always won more than we lost. We would win noodles, candy bars, even money off other guys' commissary. Kenny was a good kid. With him being twenty-something and me being thirty-something, we got along. We were able to read each other well without having to talk, which was the purpose of playing that game. I was able to make some extra money, so I could eat something else besides this crap that they served us.

We began to talk about being locked up, and we would go over the rules. They give you a rule book when you first get in, but it's just way too vague. It's always best for you to just talk to people when you're in there. Let them fill you in with the details of the ins and outs of how everything is run here.

What you don't want to do is stand in a corner and keep to yourself, because people here love to take advantage of other people when you're there. Best thing to do is stand up straight and look people in the eye when you're talking to them. Then listen to them when they are talking to you. You don't want to disrespect or get into a fight with anyone in here for sure.

Kenny and I would talk, and he would explain to me how the officers who wore white jackets and white pants were in charge over the guards who wore blue coats and blue pants. He told me if you ever have a problem with one of these guards, you would have to go get a white coat to settle out any grievances you might have.

Each guard had a different set of rules that they tried to make you follow. It was always good to talk to someone who had been there for a while. Kenny knew which guards enforced rules and which ones didn't. He had been locked up in here for over a year now, trying to get a trial date, so to him this basically was his second home. Kenny would warn me which one of the guards was letting people eat together at the table, sharing their commissary food, making a dip. He would also warn me about the other guards sending guys to the lockdown room for a day because of it.

I used to watch these guys get so crazy over these dips that they would make in there. The inmates would put all their commissary together and make something out of it. Most of the time it would be made of ramen noodles, a part of a summer sausage, chopped-up pickle, and some Flamin' Hot Cheetos. Then they would add a whole bunch of different other things depending on who was making it. After that, they would put it on a tortilla and make a burrito out of it.

It ended up being this huge pile of mush, which they would wrap up in little burritos. Everyone seemed to like them. I had never tried one personally. I didn't want to share my food or put my food together with anyone else's, so I never had the pleasure of trying one. I didn't want these guys handling my food in any way. Some of them had long fingernails with a crazed look in their eyes. I didn't want any of those guys being around or handling my food. I just said, "That's okay. I'm good."

I would watch to see who was taking advantage of, and who wasn't. Some guys got away with not spending too much money, while other people almost spent everything that they had feeding the other inmates in there. There seemed to be a hierarchy like when witnessing a group of monkeys in the jungle. The guy who was cooking was always second-in-command, and the boss directed the whole show by gathering and getting people interested and invested in that night's cook.

I was usually too busy for all that nonsense. I was good with my ramen noodles and Ritz Crackers. It was a cheap and easy meal that would keep me from going hungry. I had other things that were keeping me busy. I usually had a letter I was in the middle of writing or drawing that I was working on for Olivia. Kenny came over to the table where I was writing a letter to Tammy one day.

He asked, "Did you hear about the work program?"

I said, "No."

He said, "Get this, if you don't have anything violent in your background, you can apply to work in the kitchen or maintenance." With only $20 to my name when I came, and whatever money I did have on the outside I left with Tammy, I needed a way to make money here fast. The food that they were giving us was not cutting it.

Kenny and I signed up. I was thinking, *My wife isn't going to give me any money locked away in this place with my daughter at the house.* In the letter I was writing, I told her I would be signing up for a job in the kitchen. Then I told her to give Olivia a big kiss for me. With each letter I wrote to her, I signed them with XOXOs, meaning hugs and kisses. I also wrote to her saying my mom wasn't going to front me the cash for bail, so I might be in here for a while.

After waiting a few days, I found that I did end up qualifying for the work program. Later I found out that I would be working in the kitchen. Kenny found out that with his background the way it was, he didn't qualify. After that, I made a few phone calls to my family asking them to please help Tammy out with money while I was here. I also told them I would be okay with money from now on while I was here, that I would soon be working.

Classification ended up moving me out of the pod that I was in and ended up moving me to the fourth floor. I would be washing dishes for 25¢ an hour was what they told me. At least I had something to do. I got sent to the working deck, which was on the other end of the facility. When I walked in, I immediately noticed it smelled a whole lot better in there than the last pod that I had just come from. The walls were freshly painted. It had one big bunking quarters, which also had twice as thick mattress that felt like a cloud compared from the last mattress downstairs.

This working pod had thirty or so guys bunking together in one big room. It did have a rec room with six TVs, and two of the six TVs had PlayStation on them. They also had the hottest water in the jail for cooking, so it had its perks. With the little free time I had, I would watch TV. But each of the TV was on a different channel, and it was always kind of hard to listen to. The Mexicans had their Spanish channel. The blacks had their BET channel. And the whites mostly watched cop shows. Man, cop shows—it's the last show I wanted to watch in here. But when I did, I would find myself rooting for the bad guy every time. I would find myself yelling at the TV, "No, not that way. Go the other way" to get away from the police, which they rarely did.

We all pretty much watched the news in the morning. I would be watching a lot about Africa and all these Africans dying from an Ebola outbreak over there. I remember them saying that this could turn into a devastating global pandemic if it spread to other countries. The media would switch right back in talking about what was going on in Hollywood at the time. The news really pissed me off back then too. You had your basic local news stations. But with only two or three world news organizations, the only news that you would get at the time was what was going on in Hollywood. It seemed like the government liked to just keep the public distracted and in the dark about anything that was going on in this world. I always wondered why they never talked about real news. I wanted to know more about Ebola.

Some of the people in there were just crazy, mostly drug addicts. It seemed like the drug dealers always had enough money to sit comfortably in their cells, while the addicts and thieves were always stuck with no money to speak of. Most of the time, they had to work in the kitchen to earn extra money for the essentials like soap and coffee and extra food, which seemed like you would continually need. I was always hungry in there.

The people whom I really felt sorry for were the people who were locked up in solitary. There were fifty to sixty guys per night—broke, stuck, eating this food with no snacks to speak of. Their only entertainment was the Bible to read until they were able to leave. We would make their food and put it on rubber trays, and instead of a fork, they would have a cardboard spoon to eat with. I felt lucky to be in a place like this even though they worked me like a slave.

The people who got put in here for shoplifting would tell me how they stole things like clothes and different items from department stores. They told me they would look for events that would cause a riot and go around taking advantage of people and businesses while these events were going on. Then after that event was over, they would sell those items on the streets to make a living.

This one guy said he would hit work trucks and steal all their tools, then sell them down the street from where they stole them. I thought, *What a way to make money.* I couldn't understand why it didn't occur to these people to just get a job. I had fallen victim to one of these guys in the past when I had a job in Chicago, and I remember getting so angry that I had let my insurance lapse on my tools. I don't think some of these guys think of what happens when they commit these kinds of crimes against people. Personally, I don't think they care or have any empathy at all.

Trying not to think about it, considering I was looking at a lot more prison time than many of these other inmates for a stupid driving offense, back to work I went. I would wake up at six in the morning every day to work in that jail kitchen and not get back until six in the evening. It was getting old. They sure were getting their 25¢ an hour out of me.

I remember always being so irritable because I couldn't smoke here. Man, I needed a cigarette. There were always guys in there who would sneak one now and then when they took out the garbage in the kitchen. When they would ask me, I always said no. I didn't know what would be worse, taking a drag or two from a cigarette every day or just quitting.

I always felt as if I was trying to crawl out of my skin in here, rooming with thirty or so other guys; and somebody was always up to something, getting up out their bed, talking or coughing up a third lung, when I was trying to get some sleep. Then there was the snoring. God help me, it sounded like a group of competing circular saws going off every night.

I did feel sorry for this one kid who came in. He had this short black hair. The skinny white kid couldn't have been more than five feet and two inches and 110 pounds, soaking wet. I think his name was Shane or something. This poor kid looked more like a girl than a guy. I could tell he would get picked on constantly in here.

I would always stick up for Shane, though. The other inmates would take his lunch and harass him for how feminine he looked. Shane said he was in a band, and he said he could get me some good old-school acid when he got out. We exchanged numbers and agreed we would hook up after we got out. Shane was not much help in the kitchen, always hiding somewhere. I would catch him and said to him, "If one of these other guys catches you hiding from work in here, you are going to feel a world of hurt. Just letting you know, don't come looking to me to save you if these guys catch you."

There were a lot of people I met in there, always with a sob story telling people how innocent they were and how they didn't deserve to be in there. But man, they mostly all worked hard as if their lives depended on it. Something about getting off drugs and alcohol turned these guys into hard workers. It seemed as if they were trying to prove themselves worthy. For me it just made the time go by. They always seemed to share their opinion on how everything should be done, though, which got kind of annoying. If their ego didn't get in the way, they all seemed to be happy just to be doing something to keep their minds from being locked in here. I would try to think that we were working on the outside somewhere and these guys were my coworkers, which basically they were. For the most part, we all got along fine.

Doing the dishes was the worst. Everyone who came in there had to make their start in the kitchen doing dishes. That person would then rotate and do something else when a new guy came in. You would have to get suited up every day with a long trench coat and a protective plexiglass face mask because after you banged out the food from the tray into the garbage, you would have to spray off whatever remaining food that was on there with this high-powered hose. The little pieces of food would come back and hit you in the face. It was pretty gross.

The head chef was funny over there. He was a skinny black guy. I believe his name was Mitch. He gave me respect. He was cool. He would continuously be complaining all the time about white people in there, though. Even in front of me, one of the only white guys who were working down there at the time. He always would be talking on how white people stole their music and all their ideas. He would just go on and on. I figured I had to say something. So I said, "Well, what about *The Wiz?*"

He said, "*The Wiz?*"

"Yeah, *The Wiz*. That movie where they came up with all black cast playing parts in *The Wizard of Oz*.

"Oh yeah, I remember *The Wiz*," he said.

That was the thing when I was in there. You can't get offended when you were there, because that would just get you in trouble. You just had to have thick skin and take everything that everyone said in there in stride. Then come back with a comment and try not to sound racist, which was hard sometimes; but if you were telling the truth and made a joke out of it, the high tension in the room would go away, and all of us could share a laugh.

There were eight to ten inmates down there at any given time. They always had anything sharp locked on a chain, but if someone wanted to find something to stab me with, I'm sure that they would come up with something. So even though the guys seemed nice enough, I was always looking over my shoulder and trying not to anger anyone while I was in there.

The cooks always seemed to have a problem with mice in the kitchen. One morning, when we walked in, the cash register for the guards was left open. All the mice in that kitchen turned the money that was in the cash register into paper-mache. Mitch came up to me with these wide eyes and the crazy-like moves that he used when he was mad about something. With his hands in the air, he said, "They ate the money, man. They ate the damn money, man."

"What? What money?" I said.

"The mice. They ate the money, man. I must have left the register open," he said.

I looked into his office, and there were little ripped up money pieces all over. Mitch said he figured they lost a little over a thousand dollars that morning. I wasn't much help. I couldn't stop laughing at him. The way he said it. See, he had this Chicago style mixed in with some southern Cajun accent, which just made it funnier. We would joke around back upstairs for the longest time over that one. One of the guys would say that "they ate money, man. They ate the damn money, man." It was an inside joke that we would all be laughing at for the time we were in there.

CHAPTER 2

The Rumor

I believe I was on the work deck for about two months when I overheard three guards talking about the death of an officer. They were talking about a high-ranking officer named Holt who committed suicide the night before. This one guard was talking to this big white guy with a sleeve of tattoos going up his arm. He was the type of guy you would maybe see in a prison yard in the movies, but he was a riot guard policeman who wore a different kind of outfit from our typical day guard. So it was unusual to see a big, tough guy like that upset. I was the only guy in the rec room at the time, cleaning up early in the morning. I really couldn't tell if they knew I could overhear their conversation or not, but he went on to say, "Did you hear what the suicide note said?" the muscle bond guard asked. "It said the reason he did it was because of his family. What do you think he meant by that," the riot policeman with a sleeve of tattoos said to the other two guards in the room who had a confused look on their faces.

I had a good idea what that comment meant. It was most likely because of the people he worked with. I thought to myself, *What a shame.* I had a few conversations with the guy myself, and he didn't seem like the type. He would be always joking around with us, never acting superior or above me in any way. He just didn't strike me as the type of guy who would do that to himself.

When I made a noise with my broom, they turned around and noticed that I was in there with them. That's when they quickly stopped talking. I just stayed looking at the floor that I was cleaning.

I didn't ask any questions about him to any of the guards even though I wanted to, but personally I didn't care. I had a lot more important things to worry about. Trying not to think more about Officer Holt, I went downstairs to the sink to wash more dishes. That's when one of the lower-ranking cooks approached me. I think his name was Matt. He got paid professionally just like Mitch did, and he heard everything that went on in this jail. I think he forgot too sometimes that I was just an inmate in there as well.

Matt came up from behind me and said, "Hey, Sam. Did you hear about Officer Holt?" I nodded. "I bet you didn't hear about that girl who was found dead in her cell a couple of days ago with three different types of DNA in her."

"No, I didn't hear that," I said.

He said, "Damn, when word of this gets out, and when they start making the connections with that girl and Officer Holt, you're going to see how crazy this place is going to get with the press. The media is going to have a field day. All the news organizations will be going crazy over here, I'm sure."

My eyes got big, and I was starting to get pissed off thinking which one of these guards would have done that to a girl in there. "Do you think this girl got raped in her cell, then maybe killed by some of the guards in here?" I asked.

"Either that or she committed suicide afterward."

"Do they know which guards did it?"

"Yeah, but…" He said that he didn't know for sure. The DNA testing results hadn't come in yet.

"That's so crazy," I said.

After that, I tried to just shake it off, and I went back to work, trying not to think about what I had just heard. It was probably just a rumor, but coming from the people who were employees of the jail, how could it not be true? It was all too much. I had a lot going on myself with my case and all. I had a public defender, and he was pressuring me into making a deal with the prosecuting attorney. I miss my daughter. I've been talking to Tammy over the phone, and she's been missing me as well. I wanted to go home. I was thinking, maybe what with me being a model worker in the kitchen, they would take it easy on me and all.

The prosecutor was going full attack mode on me and wanted six years DOC (Department of Corrections) time. After about three months of being locked up, going back and forth from court, all this time my public defender was telling me if I plead guilty, I would only serve a year compared to six years if I took it to trial and I was found guilty. It seemed like a good idea at the time considering I didn't have money for a bond or a good lawyer. Anything to get me away from the snoring and this crazy place with everything that was going on.

The only catch my public defender says is that I would have to attend a treatment program while I was there. But if I signed up for it right away, I could finish it on the inside before I left. That's sounds like a good deal I think. He sounded so convincing. I didn't have to spend money and find rides to these stupid meetings on the outside. Plus I wouldn't have to pay any fines when I got out, which was around $10,000. I said "fine," what with me being here for almost three months. I took the deal, and they started the paperwork to get me on the next bus to Statesville prison in Springfield where I would start my journey.

I remember starting to go a little crazy around this time, singing to the guards as they were getting me ready to get shipped out to prison. "They come to take me away haha. They come to take me away hoho" as I danced before them as they opened the door to my cell. It's an old crazy song about a man going to the psych ward after his wife left him. It seemed I was doing some fortune-telling because little did I know how accurate that song was. Without saying anything, the guard smiled and nodded his head as if he was agreeing with me.

The guard took me and put me in handcuffs and into the back of a paddy wagon with three other guys for the four-hour trip to Statesville prison. His paddy wagon was a pickup truck that had a cap with dividing walls that kept us from hurting each other. It was crammed in there, and my long legs didn't have the room to stretch out, so I sat cross-legged, what with it being the only position I could fit in when I sat down.

Statesville is a prison where every prisoner in the state must go to get assisted so they can know where to send you. This was around the time when prisoners were getting time off their sentences. That's when I heard for the first time the term *good time*. This is where, if you were serving less than a year in prison, you would dress in and dress out, then go home. If this was your first time in the joint, you would get crazy time off your sentence even if you had a murder or rape charge. It was a confusing time. So I had no idea how long I was going away for.

There always seemed to be someone whom I would run into who would give me their opinion about what good time meant. But I was always met with conflicting stories. This guy I was sitting next to in the paddy wagon said I would go to Springfield to the Statesville prison, then do some paperwork, and I would just be sent back home, which they called dressed in dressed out. There was another guy saying no, that I would be spending two years in prison just like what the courts had said. The whole thing was confusing, and I had no idea what to tell my girl when we talked over the phone for the last time before I got into this sardine can that I was currently in.

By the time we finally made it to Statesville, my legs were so numb from the lack of room and not being able to move that when I stood up, my legs buckled; and I fell to the ground after getting out from the back of that paddy wagon. When I stood back up, I shook off my numb legs, and I looked around outside. The view was something out of an old prison movie. It was very old and very big. Four big complexes on a hundred or so acres of land. It had your typical tall fences and sharp razor wire. With five eight-story-tall watchtowers.

On the sidewalk leading up to one of the buildings stood a couple of old, disheveled-looking guys sweeping up poop that the seagulls had left. The guys looked creepy but seemingly happy as they worked. When I got inside, I saw that it consisted of six long hallways, five levels high, with an opening in the center, with no windows, just a whole lot of fluorescent light. It housed around two thousand people per hallway.

I was cellies with some of the strangest people in that little eight-by-ten cell that they put me in. One was cleaning the room all day, following me around wherever I went. But he was the one who had a cold, so he was constantly blowing his nose, making nasal sounds and leaving tissue paper everywhere he went. It was a good thing he was only there for a couple of days because I was about to kill him.

My next roommate was okay. He showed me how to play chess with some of the other prisoners who were locked away in their cells. There was a made-up chessboard made of cardboard from four milk cartoons and chess pieces molded from tissue paper. The guy had a talent for molding these little chess pieces. He would mold these pieces from toilet paper, water, and soap and then let them dry. He had the king, queen, and pawns laid out on this little cardboard with the acerate lettering of the board and everything. I was kind of impressed with it. The yelling got annoying, though. He would continuously be yelling through the little crack underneath the door, what with it being our only way for anyone to hear us. "Knight B4 takes rook B9!" Then an inmate from the next floor picked up the numbers where he had moved.

Yeah, the yelling and screaming in that place were something out of an insane asylum. It was hard to sleep. The guy I was rooming with taught me how to wet tissue paper and put it into your ears to make a mold, then how to use them as earplugs after they dried. There was a lot of that in there. Crazy little different ways they did to make the time go by faster and a little easier. You could tell that most of the people who were in there had been there before, so I was always willing to listen to these guys for advice.

But yeah, the only thing that they give you in that place was one pair of clothes, a toothbrush, and the King James Bible. I was getting bored enough, so I picked up the Bible and began to read it. Funny, when I opened it up for the first time with my thumbs flipping through the pages, I just so happened to turn to the page that read, in big letters, "SAMUEL." *That's a weird coincidence*, I thought. I don't know if it was a lack of sleep, but I swear whatever random passage in that book that I read seemed to be speaking to me personally. I'm not a religious guy or anything, far from it. I did take communion, and I was baptized Catholic but hadn't been to church since. There were some strange stories and sayings in that book that I never knew existed. I don't remember what I read. But it did seem whatever passage I chose to read, I understood it and made more sense to me. It was almost like it was meant for me to read it.

From that moment on, I felt like something, or someone, was guiding me; and it stayed with me throughout my stay. I didn't know if I liked that or not. I never connected to any Christian speakers in the past, but I felt as if some true magic was going on with the voices in my head that I was hearing. It was kind of spooky. I'm still uncomfortable telling anyone this. I didn't want anything to do with religion. I just wanted something to read.

About a week or so after that, the guards called me out and led me to a shower where they also gave me a change of clothes. I thought it was going to be good for me to be under a shower, but with no temperature control on it, that shower water seemed like it was five hundred degrees. You would think that the shower would be colder than usual out of fear of lawsuits. But with no temperature gauge, it just came out scalding hot.

After I changed my clothes, the guards led me downstairs where I would fill out a form asking me what my religion was. I just put down *none*, not knowing that I would be wearing a name tag that read, "Samuel Cole" and under religion it read, "none." I had to wear that name tag every day on my shirt from that day on.

They shipped me out with twenty or so other guys on a bus to Jacksonville. At least I would be taking care of this court mandate, I thought. They had a treatment center there, so I could at least get this court mandate out of the way. They ended up putting me on a bus, and off to prison I went.

CHAPTER 3

Jacksonville

After a couple of hours sitting on this bus, my ass was telling me that I needed to stand up. Luckily for me, one of the guys called out that we had arrived. We were now in the prison town, and the town was called Jacksonville as well as the prison. It was a little community in southern Illinois, close to St. Louis.

Going through the town, I saw planes spraying their pesticides over fields of corn. It looked cool considering how close the plane was to our bus. Then when we got into the town itself, there were people playing volleyball at the local bar and kids in the streets roller-skating. It did seem like I took a trip back in time going through that town. When passing people in the streets, I could tell they knew all too well what that bus meant, that there were convicts inside and they were going across town to the prison. The looks and evil stares that the people gave to us sitting in that bus were surreal, like we were scum on the bottom of their boots or something. Their mouths opened; kids dropped what they were doing and pointed at us.

When we finally got there, I got out and was met, not by the warden like you see in the movies, but by a huge black inmate with a big smile on his face. He told us the ins and outs of the prison. He told us about all the programs there, the work camp, the drug program, all the different school classes. He seemed nice enough, but I could tell that there was something behind that smile that I didn't want anything to do with. When people, especially convicts, smile too much like that, it creeps me out. He got to talking about the ways to earn time off your sentence by getting involved with these programs.

It was all confusing. I just wanted to get something to eat. Luckily, it was around lunchtime, and they were sending us to the cafeteria This complex was so big with an even bigger skyline, with cornfields and wheat fields for as far as your eyes can see. They had these little white rabbits running all over what with it being a nice spring day. It didn't seem like a prison at all until you saw the razor wire. The rabbits seemed to be comfortable to just hang out over there. Funny, they didn't seem to be afraid of anybody. The prisoners fed them constantly, so they were always kind of on the plump side of what a rabbit should look like. The prisoners all wore these light-blue outfits with white undershirts that resembled an auto mechanic uniform.

After lunch, a guard put me and four other guys in one of the eight buildings that were there. All the buildings had entrances that were in the middle of two prison wings with two guards sitting in the front desk in the middle. After you walked through a double set of doors, every time that you passed them, you would have to yell out your prison number so they could tell who was coming and going.

Now there was a door to the left and a door to the right. The right wing was the drug program where I thought I was going to. But I was sent to the door to the left where everyone was waiting to get in. I guess the program was overcrowded, and you had to wait your turn to be let into the program.

When I took a glance through the window, there were mostly all white kids, clean-cut with their shirts nicely tucked in. But they sent me to the door on the left opposite to that wing to wait to get processed in. Now this wing was mostly all black and Hispanic guys. There were some white guys too, but this room seemed to be a lot less structured, with most of the inmates not even wearing shirts, laughing about and dancing around to a new music video they were watching on one of the two TVs in the rec room.

The rec room was the first room I walked through. It had an open shower to the left that had ten or so showerheads and a hallway with six bunk rooms straight ahead. Each room has ten bunk beds with twenty prisoners to room. They led me to room 5-6 A, which was one of the ten bunk beds in the room. And when it said A after your number, that meant you would be on the top bunk. The top bunk was always such a pain to get up and down from. There was no ladder, so you would have to grab your utility box and turn it on its side every time so you could get up and down from the bed even as tall as I was.

Talking with the people there was pretty interesting. Some had strong southern accents. Some seemed very educated, telling me how they would deal with my case if they were me, and some others talked as if they were from the south side of Chicago with an Ebonics dialect, yelling at me and each other all day. They would consistently be telling me how I was doing this or that wrong. When I should or shouldn't be taking a shower or use the bathroom. Depending on who I was talking to, it always changed. Most likely, it was just a way to test my patience and to see how much shit I would take. I was always doing something wrong according to these southside guys. I never wanted to start anything, so I just nodded and stood my ground and let it roll of my chest. I always tried to make a funny comment so they would stay off my back, what with it being my only defense.

This one guy who had a southern accent was always talking to a South-Side-of-Chicago guy about doing and selling drugs. They made me laugh. It just seemed very unlikely that they would get along with each other. But they did, talking together and hanging out all day. I found myself hanging out with these guys when I was there. They were bunkmates two beds down from mine. We would play cards together, what with it being the best way to pass the time. The guy from Tennessee would tell me he quit smoking crack and started using heroin. With his southern drawl he said to me, "I got tired of looking out windows, so I fell asleep." Then he told me that's how he got busted at a traffic light sleeping. That guy cracked me up.

I was housed with the most different actors that you could put together. These rectangular rooms had twenty bunk beds, ten to a side, and a hallway down the middle. There were no doors. It was kind of scary falling asleep in there from a fear that you were going to be attacked when you slept.

For the most part, we all got along. I think that was a better way to go than keeping all the races segregated. I was outnumbered, what with me being the one out of three white people in that room. It had ten black guys and seven Hispanic guys. We were forced either to get along or fight. Believe me, it was a lot easier to just try to get along. And we did for the most part.

There would be times when these guys would keep me up, rapping all night and coming up with new lyrics for their songs. There always seemed to be someone who was going to be the next up-and-coming rap star. It got annoying. However, at times, it was funny. This one kid had come up with a rap that sounded like the bear in the movie *The Jungle Book*. I let him have it and told him so. The other guys laughed, and he finally sat down.

There were others who seemed to never agree on sports stats, yelling at each other constantly about who was right and who was wrong. That got annoying as well. The people who had a TV in their bunk didn't seem to be bothered by the yelling since their earbuds were connected to the TV. So that's all they heard. I was jealous they didn't seem to hear a thing.

When I finally got to lie down and get some sleep, and I had a crazy dream. I dreamt I was on a plane trying to stop a terrorist from blowing up the plane. The dream seemed so real. I woke up scream-ing, "It's a bomb! It's a bomb!" I woke everyone in the room up. You can say I was not the most popular guy in the room that night. While some of the guys laughed it off, others got pissed. "Sorry, guys," I said. The guy with a strong southern accent said, "Damn, Cole, you scared the shit out of me." I said, "Sorry, guys" with a crackle in my voice. I put my pillow over my face to hold in the laughter till I fell back asleep. The way these guys with southern accents talked was so funny. They had a long drawl to whatever they said, which took that much longer to say it. At least I wasn't the only one in the room who was laughing. I felt sorry for the guys who wanted to get back to sleep.

After waiting in this wing for about a week, I found out that all you need is to be waiting in this wing to get into the program to get six months off your sentence. You don't necessarily need to be in the program. They had all sorts of different activities to get time off your sentence. Some buildings had school courses, and other buildings had work courses, meaning if you had computer experience, you got to work in the main office to do work for the prison. Each building separated us all under different classifications, and there were six buildings in total.

I always thought it was funny. These people are probably never going to acquire a job like that when they leave, being a felon and all. Why not teach about a physically demanding job? This whole place was confusing. I just wanted to go home as fast as possible. I just missed my baby girl's first birthday, and my wife was having a hard time making it without me. I still had this drug treatment mandate looming over my head. I really needed to get that done while I was here.

After waiting there for a couple of days, I found out I didn't end up getting into the drug program from overcrowding, so they sent me to the work camp across town. Picking up garbage off the highways, I thought, *Why not if I would be getting out early?* But then I asked myself, "Do I get credit for the drug treatment course?" I knew there would be no way I could drive to the class on the outside and with no way to afford it and no way to get back and forth. I knew I was in trouble.

This work camp as they called it was a fifteen-minute bus ride away. It was kind of nice to spend a lot more outdoor time playing horseshoes all day, and exercising on the weight equipment was fun. But I didn't get a chance to go to work there, because of their overcrowding there as well. The favoritism that some of the other inmates would get was silly. What with me being new and all, I had to wait my turn if I was going to work on the outside to earn any cash. Using the phone was expensive It would be nice to make any money to put minutes on my phone. The less money my family had to spend on me, the better.

There were a lot of guys in there who were taking full advantage of the phone and the compensation money their baby mommas would get being in there. I didn't know just how much they were getting, but you could tell which guys in the morning were doing it. There was a mad dash every morning to the two phones that they had, asking each one of their baby mommas for money so they wouldn't have to eat the prison food that they were serving us.

I was pretty upset when I couldn't do my treatment there. That was my whole point of going there in the first place. So I started sending slips to the counselors, trying to get me back over there. After a week or two of sending those letters every day, I must have hit a nerve because I was sitting across the table with one of the head counselors from there. She was relatively cute, but there was something weird in her eyes, though. They seemed to have white going all around her pupils like she was stressed out, or maybe she was on drugs or something. I don't know. We went over my drug and alcohol history. I told her about my family and my one-year-old daughter. She seemed to like me, so after we got done talking, she told me I would be leaving in a day or two to head back over there and start my treatment.

The next day I got woken up in the morning by one of the guards "Cole, PACK IT UP! The guards sure could yell. It seemed they all could have been a drill sergeant in the army or something. So I packed up my stuff once again and headed back to the treatment center in a bus.

When I got there, they sent me back to the building that I left two weeks ago. I walked through the front of the building, and they sent me through the right set of doors this time. I took two steps in, and I seemed to have stepped onto a different planet. There were clean-cut, mostly white inmates, about forty to fifty of them, laughing as three guys stood up in front of everyone, acting as if they were bacon. Their hands were waving up in the air with their bodies squirming around as if they were bacon. Then there was a huge, overweight woman laughing too, monitoring it all.

That's messed up, I thought to myself. *What the hell has that to do with staying sober?* Hopefully, they weren't making fun of the counselor because of her weight. It was more of a class that they made you participate in so you could go home early. To me, honestly, it looked like they were doing some sort of hazing initiation tactic. When I thought more about it, that would make me want to go out and drink even more when I left. What the hell. What in the hell did I sign up for? If the counselor or somebody else had told me this kind of stuff was going on in there, there would be no way I would be walking through those doors.

I unpacked my stuff in room 5. It was one out of the six rooms this wing had, and with twenty men to each room, you could say it was crowded to say the least. The line to take a shower or use the bathroom was always constantly long, not to mention the line to the phone. One of the inmates came up to me and introduced himself. His name was Brian. He was kind of a porky-looking fellow with a bald head. He had these red chubby cheeks, and in my head I started to laugh. He kind of reminded me of an overgrown baby as I was listening to him talk. Well, anyway, he was saying that he was my designated buddy as they called it, that he would be there for me if I had any questions about the rules and regulations or what was going on at any given time.

"Hey, Brian," I said to him, "what in the hell was that?"

"What?" he said.

"What I just walked through."

"Well, every morning and evening we have meetings, games, and discussions about addiction and treatment."

"Well, that's fine and dandy," I said. "But what's with the public display of humiliation? Making those guys do little dances in front of everyone."

He said with a smile on his face, "That form of treatment came from the gateway program that everyone had to do." He said that they did it to relieve themselves from any kind of anxiety from standing up in front of a crowd.

"What that would cause me to have more anxiety than anything," I said.

"Well, at least you're getting out of those rooms where they room you with all the black and Hispanic inmates. Everyone in here is white."

"I see that. If this is the price I have to pay, I want nothing to do with it."

Then Brian said, "It's not so bad in here. They have a couple hot counselors here. Just do what they tell you, then you can go home early up to six months before your release date." I told him about the court mandate and that I wasn't there for the early release.

"Funny, I can see where you're coming from. You're here on a court order to fry like bacon. Funny," he said.

"What the hell," I replied.

The first night in there was crazy. The guys have this one mattress nobody liked, and the new person always ended up with it. Since I was the new guy, I got it. It was horrible. The mattress was lumpy and hard, just a complete mess. So I ended up just sleeping on the steel frame for the first night; at least it was flat. Sleep? I did not get much at all that night.

The next morning, without getting much sleep the night before, I told myself I had to do something. I took apart the whole mattress, trying to flatten it out. When I pulled it apart, I noticed it was filled with asbestos. The reason I noticed was because of doing all those remodels for my construction company.

After my introduction to the program, I immediately stuck out like a sore thumb, not participating with any of their group mentality insanity. So I took a slip of paper from the ticket box without anyone seeing. That's when I was taught the power of writing out a ticket. I wrote one to the whistleblowers that policed the police in there. When I wrote the letter, I sent it as an anonymous letter telling them about the asbestos mattress. That mattress was gone that night. All the guys were wondering where my mattress went. And why and how I got a new one. I played dumb and said, "I have no idea."

I thought, *Okay I will have to put up with this program for two to three months like my lawyer said. Then I'll be out.* "How long is this program for?" I asked.

Brian came back at me saying, "Four months."

"Four months?" I said. "Well, I'll be out in two." See, in my head, with this good time they were giving out to first-time offenders, I thought I had to be a candidate for the program. He told me he didn't know about that, but he told me that if you leave or get kicked out, the punishment is harsh. He told me they would make you serve your whole sentence with no other good time that you could qualify for. How could they do that? I thought maybe he was giving me a line. How could they mess with your release date like that? But I talked to some of the other guys, and they all said the same thing.

They had these meetings twice a day and always led with some crazy chant everyone would have to say in unison before each one started. This place was messed up. It was very structured with a whole lot of crazy rules. It kind of reminded me of a Hitler youth war camp. Everyone was dressed the same. Shirts had to be tucked in; everyone had assigned jobs. There were four guidance counselors, two of them extremely overweight. One of them was kind of cute, but this was certainly not the place. It wasn't hard to make my cute list in there. After all, I hadn't seen a woman who wasn't suited up in tactical gear in about six months. However, this place was not for me. This place kind of pissed me off. But I couldn't leave because of the court mandate. And they couldn't kick me out for not doing what they told me to do 'cause of the mandate, so I was stuck. And they were stuck with me.

I started going a little crazy while I was in there. I had been there for over a month. With the anger I felt and the lack of sleep, I started to lose it. I started reading the King James Bible again when I was in there. The guys and I were getting along, but there was no way I was going to go through what they were going through to get out of there early, so there was a disconnect, and I found myself making fun of them.

So I tried to stay as quiet as I could by reading the Bible, what with it being the only thing I had to read in there. For some strange reason, the passages seemed to make a lot more sense to me when I was locked up. The passages when you read them are left wide open to interpretation, which could mean two or many different things. When I was studying, I was always looking for some kind of hidden meaning behind whatever I was reading. It was weird; I felt as if I was getting a download of information every time I read it. I picked up the book, and the voices in my head were growing stranger and louder too.

I was writing slips to these women counselors in there saying I felt as if I was in some sort of cosmic push or something, like I was meant to be there. After reading some Bible passages, I would be getting these strange déjà vu feelings too. It was creepy, like I was in a movie that I watched before.

So they made me come in and talk to one of these girls about it. I literally broke down and told her there was a cosmic external force that was pushing me to be there. That I was being used as a tool and that I wasn't going to participate in their program. See, they knew that couldn't kick me out with this court mandate, so I was making everyone nuts in there, including myself. This poor girl looked as if she had just gotten out of college. She didn't know what to say. She just wrote everything I had to say down in her little notebook. Then she told me she would be recommending me to see a psychiatrist. "That's fine," I said and left the room.

At least I had my mom over the phone. She seemed to agree with me that maybe this program was not for me. I was talking to her a lot about what they were trying to teach us in there. At least I had her. We would laugh and talk about the things they were making these guys do. I would get into deep conversations with her about ego and social science. I would tell her, "The only way I was going to stay sober on the outside is going to be out of an act of sacrifice for my daughter." I would tell her that they were telling me it's a selfish program and the only way to stay sober is if you do it for yourself. I'd been a part of the AA program in the past, and they always said the same thing. It always seemed so selfish to me. I told my mom I was going to try something different this time. And that the only way it was going to work for me was if I was going to do it out of sacrifice.

I would try to tell the other counselors this, and they would disagree with me. They said, "No, you must stay sober for yourself." I would tell them that didn't make much sense to me. "It's not a selfish program. It's a selfless program," I would say. See, their teachings came right out of textbooks of Alcoholics Anonymous. When they went to their fancy colleges, that's what they were taught in their psychology courses. I could kind of see where they were coming from, trying to pay off their tuitions and all. They didn't want to hear me out. See, I don't think they ever had to try to overcome an addiction problem like we did. Well, in my opinion, maybe they should.

I was kind of thinking about what the difference between my addiction and theirs was, how they would feel if they got sent to prison for eating behind the wheel, which should be outlawed as well in my opinion. They are endangering themselves and their kids if they are teaching them it's okay to eat that way. I would like to see them stand in front of everyone and act as if they were frying, as if they were bacon, so they could get out of prison early to get back to their kids. This place just didn't make any sense. I still wanted to drink, and nothing was going to change that.

I said to them one morning in a group, "I'm going to start living my life as an act of sacrifice for the people in my life and for my daughter." Then they said to me, "No, you must do it for yourself." I told them I tried that before, and it didn't work for me. Then I said to the group, "You see, it's all about the sacrifice you make for your kids. Okay, let's go. Let's see how far down that rabbit hole really goes." They all kind of looked at me with these wide eyes like I was nuts.

Around this time, the news was talking heavily every day about Ebola and how it might spread to other countries with more than fifty thousand already dead in Africa. Then there was a story about Tony Stewart (race car driver) running over another driver on a dirt track, and it was caught on film. That's the first time I saw it. The events that were shown on TV had changed. It had a particular anger that I didn't recognize. It was if I sensed a sort of evil that was coming out of the screen. This driver got mad, and when he got out of his car, Tony ran him over accidentally in the middle of the race, and he died.

I think there was something on the news about Michael Brown and how black people were mistreated by white cops. So I started talking about race with one of the only black guys in this treatment center. I think his name was Thomas. I was telling him all the police would have to do was wear some sort of camera on their vests so nobody could lie about what had happened, neither the police nor the defendant. Then I got into why black people seemed to always want to fight with the cops and run. They never seemed to get away with it. They just made it harder on themselves. Then Tomus came back at me saying, "They don't show the ones who got away from cops. Think about it," he said.

"Maybe you're right," I said. "If you act like you're doing nothing wrong, there is more of a chance that you will get away with it."

Tomus said, "Not if you're a black man. Maybe it's just what they're showing me on TV, and the media is cherry-picking."

Then I said to him, "If you just stay chill and play dumb, nine times out of ten, they have to let you go."

"Not if you're black. You just don't know what kind of cop you are going to be in contact with, a normal one or someone who mediately gives you attitude."

"If I were a cop, there would be no way that I couldn't be part of some sort of racial profiling. I would have to just stay alive. Being downtown at night in an all-black neighborhood where there are people getting murdered every night, how you could not? I would be scared to death."

"True," Tomus says.

I just about had enough of this program, watching these guys doing dances for these women. I don't know why I was so offended. I wasn't the one doing the dancing. It didn't seem like anyone else was offended. I bet most of them were just glad to be out of the general population and with a promise of being let out early. To me it seemed like a hazing ritual more than anything to get out of there early. I think they knew that, though. I don't think this place was designed to help anyone. It was a way for the prison system to have a constant flow of inmates for the money. When I started to think about it, it started to make more sense. Then I started to get a sense of what this whole thing was about, and I started to make all these connections in my head.

I was reading the Bible a lot and talking on the phone with my mom about social science and ego. Then I started to talk about something that seemed so familiar in all of this, and I was experiencing a lot of déjà vu. "Something weird was going on in here, Mom. I don't know what it is, but it almost feels like this all has a biblical feel to all of this."

Somone must have been listening to my recorded phone conversation, or my counselor's recommendation came through because an hour after I was talking to my mom, one of the guards gave me a slip saying to go to the prison psychiatrist. It said I would go for an hour out of this wing and walk across the yard to her office. Her office had its own entryway in that building. There were a lot of other people out in the yard that day. Everyone knew if you were going through those sets of doors, you were going. I walked in. She seemed nice and asked me to have a seat.

When I talked with her, she agreed with what I had to say about the program. Then I started talking about what they were making us do in there and that if I did what they were asking me to do, I would turn to drugs and alcohol even harder, trying to forget what I had to do to get out of there. When we talked, we shared a laugh or two, then she sent me back to the woman counselors with a clean bill of mental health.

I could see I was really starting to anger some of these counselors at the time. They were asking me why I didn't tell the psychologist about the cosmic pushes and the cosmic beats I said I was feeling. I told them I said what I said to them to get it off my chest, that I didn't need to tell her about that because I had already told them.

They sent me back to my room where I was met by the guys, asking me, "Did you hear Orange Crush is here?"

"What's Orange Crush?" I asked.

"It's a militant group that is sent to prisons if a group of prisoners are getting out of control. I heard they might be coming in here and busting people up. In the last prison they sent me to, three inmates got sent to the hospital with broken bones after they got what they wanted." As he's talking to me, I was starting to think, *Are they here because of me?* I was thinking now how much trouble I was in.

After almost two months being there, they really wanted to get me out. So they came up with a plan to get me so pissed off that I would start a fight in there or quit. The warden had five huge guys dressed in orange, Orange Crush as they were called, waiting outside the building as they put this poor guy in a girly outfit. He had this tutu princess dress outfit on and stood up in front of everyone. This poor guy was one of the elders of the program. He was the one everyone went to if you had a problem. I knew the guy only had one week to go on his sentence. Man, I felt sorry for him. He had a daughter at home too, but if he didn't do what these counselors were telling him to do, then he would be labeled as someone who was not participating in the program. Then he would be kicked out of the program and serve six more months on his prison sentence. I don't think this guy had a choice.

This guy was smiling at me when he started dancing and singing,

> I'm a little teapot
> Short and stout
> This is my handle
> This is my stout
> When I get all steamed up
> Then I shout
> Tip me over and poor me out

He was dancing as a little girl would do with his hands acting if he were a teapot, dancing and singing way too close to me. I swear I was going to snap. Something happened to me. When I took a glance at him, my face started to turn red. I was about to blow up. It was if they knew what was going to set me off, and they planned this whole thing for me.

But then something came to my mind. It was something I was watching on TV the hour before. It was about that kid who got out of his car and got run over by Tony Stewart, the race car driver. It was if the TV was warning me or something. So that was still on my mind, and that was my only defense. I could not look at him, and I couldn't stand up. I had to sit there and take it.

I truly think If I had, I would have stood up and went nuts on these fat-ass counselors in there. There would have been hell to pay. But I just sat there with my head down. I had to force myself not to look. I knew if I had, that military group would have come in and messed me up for sure and maybe some of the other guys in there too. So I sat there and took it. I never looked back up until he left, and the Orange Crush never came in.

After it was all done, I went up to one of the obese counselors and said to her, "I'm okay as long as I don't have to look at it." I swear she did one of those eye-twitching things. I could see the rage behind her eyes. I had pissed her off, I could tell.

"You're out of here, Cole," she said.

"Why? What did I say?" I said with a crackle in my voice, trying to hide my fake laughter.

When I left, they moved me back to the other side of the building where I first started out a few months ago. There were people in the opposite wing to the program and supposedly waiting to be let in. Well, at least I didn't give up. Maybe they would still count this for completion since they weren't supposed to have kicked me out and all. I figured that the contract that they made me sign was still valid.

They made me sign a paper the next day after I left for my early release. After I signed it, I thought I probably shouldn't have. With all the problems that I was causing down there and the fact they used the cutest counselor there, I signed it. I'm such a sucker for a cute girl in some tight jeans. After I signed the paper, I asked if I could still be let out early with good time. She just looked at me and smiled and walked away. She got what she wanted.

Classification put me in a room where I was the only white guy. All of them seemed like the type of guys who were very proud of their race. The guys in there weren't too happy by the looks on their faces that I was going to break up their little party in there.

I was looking at these guys, and there was no way they were ever going to go through that program and fry like bacon for those white counselors either. No way, but they all were there waiting for an opening. I came to find out as long as they were waiting for an opening, their sentence would be reduced without stepping foot in that program. That was part of the deal. That's when I asked my bunkmate below me, "The warden of this prison is black, isn't he?"

"Yeah, why?" he asked.

"No reason," I said.

I thought now by putting me in there, they wanted me to beg them to be let back into their program. They would come up to me and ask me if I was ready to come back. But these guys and I got along fine. They started to give me shit in the beginning, and I saw the guy I shared a bunk with talking behind my back. So I went up to him and said, "Ha, if you have any problems with anything that I'm doing wrong, you can come up to me and talk to me about it. This is my first time here. If you wouldn't mind telling me how things work in here."

He turned to me and nodded at me, then nodded to the person whom he was talking to. Then he said to me, "Just don't stink." He said I might want to take a shower. Then I apologized and said that they were really making me sweat in there with the things that they were making people do. So I said, "No problem. I'll jump in the shower right now."

Most of the inmates in there had no idea what was going on in that program, and even if they did, they would probably not go through that torture either if they had a choice. The counselors and the warden, I believe, knew that too. But those white kids in the program were always so scared to be kicked out and get sent to the room where I was in. I got along with these guys fine. It was a lot better than dealing with those wussies.

I think this was all a setup, though. All of this had to be a plan for me to come running back to the program and comply with the things that they were making everyone do in there. I was not happy in there for the most part. There was no way I was going to go back there, court mandate or not.

Calling my girl, on the other hand, I thought, might be a different story. I was scared about what she was going to say. When I talked to her, I was surprised that she agreed with me and said that she probably would have done the same thing. She wouldn't have fried as if she were bacon for these people either. She told me not to worry. She just got a promotion at her job. We would be okay.

Then she asked if I wanted to speak to my baby girl. I said, "Of course." Olivia came on the phone, said, "Hi, Da Da," then dropped the phone; and she ran off. I could hear her little footsteps on the hardwood floor after she dropped the phone. I burst out crying. Tammy got back on the phone.

"Oh my god, she spoke," I said.

"Yeah, she misses you. She keeps on picking out books for you to read to her even though you're not here."

I tried to hold back the crackle in my voice.

Tammy said, "I love you, baby. Hopefully, I'll see you soon. Do you know when you're getting out?"

"I don't know yet." I told her it's really confusing, so hopefully sooner rather than later. "Maybe in the midsummer," I said. "They're letting people go early all the time here." We said our goodbyes and hung up the phone. After my phone conversation, I shook it off and tried not to get caught by the guys with all these tears running down my face. I jumped on a TV no one was watching.

Michael Brown's death was posted all over the news around this time. There was a white cop from Ferguson who shot Michael Brown, a black man, outside a convenient store. The news of it was driving everyone crazy in there with Ferguson, Missouri, being only just over an hour away from there. "Racist. Racist. Racist!" all these guys would be yelling as they crowded around the second TV in the rec room that morning.

I didn't blame them considering what the news was telling them. I didn't blame the news either. All the news organizations are looking for is the ratings. I was talking to my buddy John. He was cool. He was a little calmer than the other guys in there. I told him these news channels were going to cause a riot. I said, "You know what, Michael probably did something to scare that cop for his life and left him with no other choice." Most of the guys agreed when I said that. Then the rec room got a lot quieter at least for a little while.

But it was funny how the news broadcaster started talking about cameras for cops that they would be starting to wear on their vests.

I told John that I had just talked to someone about that a couple of days ago. With all the trouble I was sure I was causing, I wouldn't be surprised if there was a camera in this TV. Maybe somebody was listening to me and collaborating with someone on the outside, maybe even the news, and getting my ideas out there. John told me there weren't any guards most of the time, and the riot police guards always seemed to know the exact right time to get in there when there was something bad going on, like a fight or something. He told me that there was most likely a camera in there somewhere.

I had been talking on the phone with my family too about this place, and I knew they recorded all these conversations. So I would start playing with them, talking about the program and how they were mistreating the inmates. Hopefully, there would be a whistleblower listening to me to get the Department of Corrections in trouble. Maybe they would start treating these inmates with some dignity and respect and stop messing with their release dates.

I would tell my mom over the phone something felt familiar about this place. It was as if I was in a movie or something. I told her to "watch this. This is going to be epic." I didn't know at the time what I was talking about. All I knew was I was mad. But my mom always calmed me down. She told me to calm down and suggested I buy a TV with the money that she had been giving me. I agreed.

Some weird stuff was going on TV around that time, even the commercials. At least now I had a TV of my own now with these earbuds. I could shut everyone out. It seemed like a good thing until I felt an ever-present evil force that was coming out of the TV. Even the shows and commercials had a hidden demonic force behind them. It could be because I was watching them in prison or with the lack of sleep I was getting. But I could sense there was a real crazy vibe I was getting from the TV. Then I was always trying to shake it off, telling myself it was from the lack of sleep. But when you had ten or so TVs going on at once in a bunk room of twenty guys, it was hard to ignore.

That went on for about a week, freaking out about the TV, when I heard one the guys yell out, "Jehovah's Witnesses are here!"

One of the guards screamed into our wing, "Church!" That means it was time that you could go and talk to a preacher from any main religion that you wanted, and this week it was the Jehovah's Witnesses' turn. Even though I hadn't been to church in a while, I always felt as if I were speaking to God but in my own way. With all the different religions to choose from, being a part of just one never made much sense to me.

So I got into this room with the two guys. They were two plainly dressed guys. One was a lot older than the other.

"Are you the only one?" the older pastor asked me. I looked behind me and nodded my head. I sat down at their table across from them. I don't know why I just started flipping out. I was so sick of these religions telling me the world was going to end. As a kid growing up in the nineties, it was kind of messed up. See, I would read books on Edger Cayce and Nostradamus. Then I would listen to all these Christian teachers talking about the book of Revelations and how in the rapture Jesus is going to be coming back to earth to save all of us so we can live for eternity in heaven. "That's it. I have had enough of it." I let them have it. I was like, "The world is going to end soon anyway, so the hell with it. I'm going to do what I want to do. As long as I believe in Jesus, it doesn't matter." I was kind of flipping out on them.

I have a two-year-old daughter at home, and I didn't want her to go through the same thing that I had to go through growing up as a kid thinking the world was going to end all the time. I was crying a little bit, and my voice started to get an angry tone to it. Then I asked, "Is this the voice of God in my head, or is it my subconscious thought?"

The older preacher said, "I don't know. But considering how serious you are, I want to show you something." Then he started to take out his Bible and turned to Revelations and pointed to a scripture and said, "Calm down. Let me read something to you. It is called a revelation for a reason. All it means is that God is going to reveal something to all of us, that's all." The world would not end. But then he said, "You must look at it as a new beginning. Here, look at this passage here, Sam. If you read here, Jesus says the meek shall inherit the earth." It didn't make much sense to me then, but it sure rings true now. I was watching the younger preacher getting mad as he was listening to the older preacher talking to me.

I said as tears were rolling down my face, "Okay, there's something on the TV that's freaking me out. I can't explain it, but I feel like there's something bad about to happen. Everything I turned on the TV, I'm seeing something in there that's not right. It is almost as if it was possessed."

"Possessed?" he asked.

"Yeah, there's an evil that is coming out of the TV that I can't explain."

"You know what," he said to me, "just turn the TV off. I feel the same way sometimes."

I thought it seemed easy for him to say that. He didn't have over a hundred TVs in a wing that I felt was watching every move I made with no way I could escape from.

I got up and said, "Thank you for your time" and walked out of there. *Helpful*, I thought, walking out of there. Why was I crying? Good thing nobody else was in there. I could hear the younger preacher laughing a little bit with the other preacher about what I had said. I was a little embarrassed of how I acted. I tried not to let anyone who passed me on the courtyard see how upset I was. I hurried up and wiped those crazy tears away. I held my head up high as I walked back to my bunk.

I got back to my room where I started writing slips to go back to the work camp so I can serve out my sentence, serving some kind of community services program. These guys were driving me nuts, yelling at each other about sport stats every night. I couldn't take being there, looking at these stupid women counselors smirking every time I would cross their path as if they won or something.

After a week or two, they sent me the slip that I was to go back to the work camp. *Cool*, I thought. Maybe there was a way to get good time after all and make it home before Christmas in eight months for my baby girl. I got all my stuff packed up, and I found out my TV order had come in. Maybe it would be a little easier to just focus on one channel on my personal TV. Hopefully, that would calm me down a little bit.

When I got back to the work camp, I found that it was on a twenty-four-hour lockdown over someone who escaped earlier that day. I introduced myself to the guys in my wing, and word got around about what I had done in the treatment center, and I was getting slack from some of the guys about it. This one guy came up to me saying that he wished he would have gotten a chance to do those dances for those ladies to get out of there early. Then I asked, "Really? Would you really?" Then he started to fry like he was bacon, which made me think if I was blowing this all out of proportion. I told him that maybe it was just me. I knew I couldn't look at myself in the mirror when I got out of there if I did the things those counselors were wanting me to do. There would be no chance that I would be sober if I left there, I told them. Doing that shit would make me want to drink even more when I left. He kind of nodded to me as if he knew what I was talking about.

This guy Carl who was also from my room was telling me we're on lockdown because there was a guy who jumped from the back of a truck and got away from one of the guards as he was picking up garbage off the side of the road. I was listening to the other guys, and they were saying that he only had eight more months on his sentence. I thought, *What would drive a man to do something like that? Take a chance of getting shot by a guard and try to escape with just eight more months to go.*

It's this place and the way that they were messing with the prisoners' sentences. I guess he went through a program like what I went through. He got denied after going almost all the way through. I guess he didn't do something right, and he had to serve out his full sentence. I almost felt sorry for him as they were loading him into the paddy wagon, watching him on my personal TV. Those two hours of freedom just cost him five to ten years more on his sentence. I think he promised his baby girl to make it home before her birthday. When he got denied his good time, he went a little nuts. To tell you the truth, I could see where he was coming from.

Man, it was hard not to watch this stupid TV in there. They were really pissing me off around this time. They were talking about putting Agent Orange, the chemical they used in warfare in Vietnam, on the corn for weed killer. What were they thinking? I was watching Dr. Oz; he was protesting it, saying it would be the worst thing ever for the health of the people, that he didn't know what people think what would happen. Putting Agent Orange on the corn just because they couldn't find a way to kill this super weed that was killing all the corn crops sounded insane to me. They said normal weed killer wouldn't work anymore, so they were going to start using agent orange.

In my next phone conversation with my mom, I was telling her about it. "Mom, did you hear about what they're about to put on the corn down here?"

"No, I didn't, Sam. What?"

"Well, I guess there's a super weed that the farmers just can't kill with their normal pesticides, and they're going to put Agent Orange on the corn to try to kill this super weed. Mom, they're going to put Agent Orange on our corn because I guess there was a weed down here that they just can't kill!" When I was speaking to her, I wasn't talking to her. My message was for the people who were listening to me on the other line.

It did remind me of what I just went through, what with me being the super weed, and a militant group called Orange Crush that was going to use brutal force to get me out of that program when I wasn't complying with the things that they were trying to make me do in there. That's when I started to laugh to myself. I could feel the presence of someone listening to my phone conversations. Maybe I was being drugged, and I didn't know. "It's in the corn," I said. "Just like the townsmen did in the movie *Children of the Corn*."

"Funny, Sam," she said. But with the tone of my voice, she couldn't tell if I was joking or not, and to tell you the truth, neither could I.

CHAPTER 4

Ticket to the Whistleblowers

The protesting and town hall meetings about Michael Brown's death were all over the news around this time. The town hall meeting in St. Louis about racial profiling would be held the next day. I was thinking, *St. Louis is just an hour away from here.* I couldn't help but to start to feel the energy; it was getting bad. As I was watching TV in the rec room, I heard one of the guards say, "Halt!" to one of the inmates as he was walking out the door.

Officer Holt. Yeah, what about Officer Holt's suicide and what he said in his note? I almost forgot about that. I was wondering why I wasn't hearing about that in the news. Maybe they're trying to cover it up. Hell, with everything that was going on in this country, I bet that's exactly what there trying to do. Something in me started to burn with anger. I needed revenge. Not only revenge for myself and every other inmate down there but for that girl who got raped and possibly killed in her jail cell.

So I wrote a ticket to the whistleblowers telling the whole story about Officer Holt committing suicide over the death of a girl in a jail cell from the county I was from. That when that girl was autopsied, there were three types of DNA in her and were put there by a few officers or guards when they raped her and then possibly killed her. And that Officer Holt, who committed suicide, may have or may not have been involved in her death.

I wanted to speak to the media. In my letter, I started it off by writing, "Stop, the bigger you make of this, the bigger this situation is going to become," circling the word *stop*. Then I went on writing that it was all the media's fault that they were trying to label us and divide us all. But it was not about labels, and it was not about race. It was about fear. Fear of people brought on by the media.

Not growing up around black people, I was always taught that inner-city black people hated me for being white. That they were mostly dangerous and aggressive and that they probably had a gun on them. That the cop wasn't a racist. He probably just got scared for his life when Michael Brown came at him all alone, aggressively. It's the training that cops went through that is making them act the way they do. They're not being taught how to defuse the situations that they're in. There was racial profiling coming from both sides, and I called it black and blue profiling.

Then I went on to write that there are different talents and abilities that a certain percentage of black people have that white people don't and vice versa. There's a lot of talents and abilities that other races have that some races do not for the most part. I'm not racist for saying so. I believe that's what makes this country so great. We all have to work together and bring all our talents and abilities to the table to make a better nation. I do believe we all must move away from this self-absorbed society we're living in into a more self-suffi-cient society I know we can become. I also put in there that I was scared to leave this prison knowing what I knew, so I when I left, I would like an escort out of there.

When I finished writing out the ticket, I put it in the ticket box and went back to my bunk. After that day was over, one of the guards was standing over my bed when I woke up the next morning. Just standing there not saying a word when I woke up. After a few seconds after I was awake, he said to me, "Are you Cole?"

I said, "Yes."

"Well, come with me," he said.

He brought me in to talk to the warden of the work camp and the nurse over there. He gave me the piece of paper I wrote the day before, and the warden asked me more about it. He seemed like a nice guy. We went into detail about Officer Holt and what I heard about what happened to that girl. That's when I asked that my letter be read aloud in the town meeting that the townspeople were holding in Ferguson about race relations. He liked what I had to say when I said that was not only black profiling but blue profiling too, meaning cops being blue from the outfits that they wore. But I started to cry again over that girl, and because I was mad of what I knew and what I heard back in my county, I might start something crazy up there and maybe in Ferguson too.

Then I started telling him my story about having to fry bacon to get out of there. That I just wanted to go home to my kid. Then he added that he could see where I was coming from with that. Like he knew all too well my situation at the treatment center the month before. I'm sure I was the talk of that town with the prison being the town's number one source of income.

I could see he was getting freaked out about how upset I was. I could see his eyes starting to get wider and wider as I took a pause from speaking. Without saying much else, he put me into another room to talk privately to the nurse. When he got out, I asked him if he was sending me to the psych ward. He shook his head no. He replied, "Don't worry, bud. We're going to sort this all out." Then I saw him getting on the phone with someone who seemed to be important based on the way he was acting. I saw him looking scared over the phone, then he would look back at me in disbelief as he was on the phone.

He sent me back to the other prison where I could speak to the psychologist again. I remember just crying a lot because I knew I was going to open up something big, and I didn't know how it was going to end. I was crying like a little girl though to one of the transport guards when he asked me, "What's wrong with you?"

I said to him, "I'm going crazy in here, but it's going to help me from going insane." He kind of stared at me for a moment, then he quickly looked away saying that he didn't know what to say to help my situation.

When I got back to the treatment center prison for the third time in three months, I immediately got sent to talk to the head psychologist there. It ended up being the same woman I talked to the month before who gave me a clean bill of mental health. I bet in foresight she was thinking she had made a big mistake. I forgot her name. But we went on and on and talked over everything I heard from the cook at the Lake County Jail I came from four months prior.

When I walked into her office, the look on this woman's face was filled with anger and fear for me. She asked me to have a seat, so I sat down on the other side of her desk. She asked me, "Where did you hear this story from?" as she was reading my letter. I told her I didn't want to name any names, but it was someone who worked in the kitchen at the jail from the county I had come from. "Well, do you know this girl personally?" she asked.

I said, "No, ma'am, but I'm sure I could look her up on the Internet to find out who she was." That kind of shut her up for a moment. I guess she was expecting a different kind of response out of me. I was thinking, *How could she be sticking up for those guards and that officer being a woman herself?*

With no denial about the story, she went on to ask if I was part of the media and if I was sent here by some news organization or something. I said no. But that's when it hit me. That story that I heard back in the county was true. This psychologist must have gotten word from one of her superiors and confirmed my story.

Then she asked, "What's this that you're scared for your life? Are you scared to leave this prison?"

"I don't know," I said. "Wouldn't you be when you almost had an encounter with Orange Crush trying get you out of that treatment center and now with this story? How am I supposed to feel?" She nodded. Then I said, "I just want to make it back home to my daughter." She then asked if it was my biological daughter, most likely wondering why I had such an intense attachment to her.

"Yes, she is, ma'am. She turned one year old, and she is my world."

She nodded and said, "Okay" with a smirk on her face. "Well, have a nice day."

I nodded back, and out of politeness, I said, "Yeah, you too" and then I left.

Have a nice day. *Have a nice day?* I was thinking as I was walking back to my bunk. With no reinsurance of my safety. With no response. No denial or telling me it didn't happen. That I must be confused about what I heard. That there was no dead girl found in a jail cell. *I'm in trouble*, I thought. Damn that was some cold shit to just send me away without telling me that no one there was going to cause me any harm while I was there. She didn't say, "You have nothing to worry about" or "don't worry, we will investigate this and thanks for notifying us." Nothing. Just "Okay, what you're thinking and your fear are justified and goodbye. Have a nice day."

The classification people in Jacksonville ended up putting me in the wing with these guys who had the worst of the worst crimes, the craziest of the crazy. Twenty guys who were the most insane guys I had ever seen. Rape, murder, robberies, holding up people at gunpoint were just a few. It really wasn't what they did. It was how they talked about it with such enthusiasm in their eyes, telling me their stories, that set me off in fear. Luckily, I was one of the biggest guys in there, and as long as I played by their rules, nothing bad was going to happen to me.

The only problem was the food that they gave us here had a lot of soy, which gave me a lot of gas. Now I did the best I could to get out of that room the fastest I could, but every once in a while, I would let one go by accident. This guy across from me—his name was Ant—let me have it one day. He came right up to my bunk, got into my face, and said, "Look, motherfucker. If you got gas, do it outside." I told him how sorry I was, that I would try harder next time. He was very big and very black. He was a guy I didn't want to mess with. He got into my face as I was lying in bed. I really didn't want to start anything in there, so I just replied that I would try harder next time.

My bunkmate Allan was always bragging, letting everyone know just how bad he was. He talked to me about the time he served in his last prison. He said he convinced his old roommate to take his own life by taking a nosedive off the top bunk into the concrete floor. What are you supposed to say to something like that? I said, "So was he an asshole or something, or was he annoying?"

He said, "No, but he was always feeling sorry for himself, and he would cry for his daughter occasionally."

"What was he in for?" I asked. Funny, he was only in there for a driving offense. He only had ten more years to go.

He would go on to tell me that he was in for murder, and he was at the tail end of a thirty-year sentence that he only had five more years to go. He went on to say that he shot a guy while he was parked in his driveway in the head. Then he talked about the brain matter being thrown all over a car. The only response I had was, "Congratulations." He smiled at me, trying to figure why I wasn't afraid of him. "What are you in for?" he asked.

I almost wanted to make up a story after I heard his. But I came back with, "My third DUI offense."

"That's it?" he said. "When's your release date?"

I said, "In ten months. But I was hoping for a good time."

"Good time? Did anyone tell you, you were getting good time, Cole?"

"No."

"Well, don't expect to get out early in here on any good time." Then he said to one of the other inmates, "Hey, John, are you getting any good time?"

I heard, "Hell no."

"Hey, Joe, how about you? Are you getting any time off your sentence with any good time?"

"Good time? Me, I'm having a great time. How about you Ant?" Ant (Anthony) just sat there with a discontent look on his face. All the other guys laughed.

Allan went on to say that there was no such thing as good time in that wing. Then he'd tell me these other stories, and forgive me for repeating this. Hopefully, whoever is reading this hasn't eaten anything recently. This guy went on and on trying to scare me, I'm sure. He told me about this guy named shit-eating Benny who would pay for other people's poop for food to maybe gross out the psychologist he was seeing at the time. But he also said he'd pay more for black persons' poop. I guess to him it tasted better for some reason. Just coming back from lunch, he was making me feel sick. I said, "Okay,

Allan, stop it. We all just came back from lunch." But he'd go on and tell me about this other guy in his last prison who ate his own eyeball too and then the next week dug out his other one and ate that one as well.

Well, they weren't too nice to me, but all in all, I held my own. It didn't stop us from joking around with each other. But still, I was the white guy. A white guy from the suburbs with a driving offense, getting out in a few months. My neighbor sleeping next to me would look at me in the middle of the night sometimes with big wide eyes. He would whisper and smile at me and say, "Sam, simple Sam, simple Sam" repeatedly and laugh. Damn, that guy creeped me out. It was almost like he was possessed by some demon who knew what I was up to in there because I felt as if I had the devil by the balls with this story, and he was using people in there to freak me out so he could create his hell on earth. I never told any of the guys what was going on. I just kept this whole story about Officer Holt to myself.

What was going on in there was epic, though. The TV at the time was going absolutely crazy. It was as if the media outlets at the time and even the president—I could swear—knew about my story. But I wasn't going to come out to say it because that just sounds crazy, but yeah, the government was militarizing the police around Ferguson with top-of-the-line tactical gear. They were gearing up for a war that, in my opinion, CNN started with their fearful and hateful speech.

The talk on the TV was all about race or anything that might be tied to race. Maybe it was all about this big solar flare too that was reacting to people on a crazy mental level. I did hear that form somewhere that even the birds get confused and weirded out when such an event occurs. All the scientists were saying to be prepared, that we were going to get hit by this thing soon.

Then these scientists who were coming back from Africa with Ebola were going to spread it to all of us. CNN was using a fear tactic to get us to fight each other or maybe an AI-generated plan to start a war on people to cut down on overpopulation. I wanted to go home and be with my daughter. I felt something really bad was going to happen. For a second, I thought maybe if I would just fry like bacon for these people, maybe they would let me go home. "Hell no! Sam, stand your ground. You got this," a voice in my head told me.

That's when I dove into books. I read about Pythagoras and how he traveled to explore all the world's religions and came back to his home in Samos and made his own religion. I would read about him talking about the only just thing a man could do for another man, which is to make sacrifices to help out his fellow man. He also talked about the true meaning of philosopher is a lover of learning, never being the wise man, and that the only thing that is worth knowing are numbers.

Reading about this guy made a lot of sense to me. I guess, according to the book, he could be in two places at once and had the ability to talk to animals, which led a lot of people to think he was creating miracles himself. They wrote something about if they found you to be worthy to join their group, then you would give up all your worldly possessions and make a vow that you would not speak for five years. I believe that book found me, not the other way around. I felt as if it was speaking to me considering what I had said back in that treatment program about the sacrifices. There were too many coincidences that were happening to call it by any other name.

Call me crazy, but I would go to the library right away. There would be something guiding me to these books. I would pick up this blue-covered Knights Templar book with their cross on the front just by chance, what with it being the first book I'd grab in this huge library. Then with the second one being a *Time* magazine hardcover book on Pythagoras. There were a series of *Time* books on different subjects. I'd tried to look up those books on the Internet recently, though, and I haven't been able to find them, so it is kind of hard to remember everything I read; but at the time I felt like what I was reading made perfect sense to me. I seemed to not have been able to put these two books down.

I found myself reading different passages in these books more than once. It seemed like everything I was talking about, like the cosmic beats, were right there before me in black and white as I was reading this book. I believe staying sober in the outside would have to be done out of sacrifice for my daughter, not for myself, which sounded selfish to me. That is what I also read, that it's all about the sacrifices.

That book also had something I read in it. Make sure to give them a war cry, which immediately made me think of a cheer that the cheerleaders sang at the basketball games in my seventh grade junior high school. "Clap your hands," then we would clap our hands three times. "Stomp your feet," then we all would stomp our feet on the bleachers three times. Then the cheer went on: "McHenry Trojans can't be beat." *That's my war cry*, I thought.

For a person who doesn't go to church a lot, I sure was getting, I felt, a download of information from a source that wasn't from this realm of consciousness. It had to be from God or gods in my opinion. The voices in my head certainly were a lot louder than I ever heard before. There was a deep connection between me and this book. I felt privileged to have been able to read it at exactly the time I needed to.

I would read about all these ancient religions in that Templar book and what they meant. Then I turned to this page that had a map on it with this long, winding road named Chaple Hill, which winded down to a road called North. *This can't be*, I thought. *What the hell. That looks a lot like a map of the 316 house I grew up in as a kid. This is just crazy. I got to get some more sleep. I got to be hallucinating.*

When I got back to the room, I started to talk to the guys about my first night there when I had a dream and woke everyone up. I was screaming, "It's a bomb. It's a bomb!" Maybe it was the spirits in that place or something. But it was making a lot more sense now. I told the guys maybe I was the bomb. "Damn, Cole, that's deep," my cellie said. Then there was this guy who was hanging out in my room. He came up to me with a smile and said, "I thought you were dead." I asked him what he meant by that. He just smiled at me and walked away. That was another thing that was happening while I was there. People would say things to me that God or the devil himself said through these people. Some spooky stuff. It took every ounce of sanity I had to not go insane while I was there.

We got word a few days later that there would be a flu shot to be given to all the inmates for the Ebola outbreak. These guys were scared, and they were attacking and harassing the guys who didn't want to get the shot. I just so happened to be one of the guys who refused.

Watching the news and watching all these people getting all freaked out about this Ebola, I decided to give my mom a call. We said our hellos and how are you doings. Then I started to talk to her about Ebola vaccines, which at the time was the flu vaccine. "Weren't they meant for the young and the old with weak immune systems? That the flu vaccine might weaken the immune system in a healthy person? Why would they give us flu vaccine for this Ebola outbreak?" I went on to tell her that the were making everyone take this vaccine in there. That there was only me and this other guy who refused.

"I don't know, Sam," she said. I told her to stay away from the vaccine. "Okay, Sam, I will," she said.

My mom was telling me my sister Tara was having a hard time after her husband, Denise, died a year before from a fentanyl over-dose. I didn't even know what fentanyl was back then. But I sure know a lot more about it now. I was starting to get pretty pissed off at the time talking to my mom about all these doctors who were getting rich as their patients were all dying of overdose of drugs like that and OxyContin. But I felt as if I wasn't talking to my mom. I was talking to the cops and guards who were listening to me on these recorded phone conversations. We need to start watching more C-SPAN instead of these stupid news channels like CNN that weren't telling us nothing about nothing. They were all trying to get us all to fight each other over these vaccines. I could tell what it was doing to all these guys in this prison. There were these guys who were pressuring me to take the shot thinking if I didn't, the whole pod might get Ebola.

Then I went on to say, "This life we have is worth fighting for." When I'd leave, I would have to ask for five years of silence. And I didn't know what the answers were, but I knew one thing is for sure—we must keep all lines of communication open! I said that knowing that there was somebody else in this prison listening at the other end of my conversation. Then I said most likely all these news organizations were not wanting us to hear the whole truth about what was really going on. Remember, it's not the way you perform; it's all about the way you serve. That's when I started to cry a little bit, then said, "It's time" and gave her my junior high war cry. "Make sure, Mom, you sing this to Tara and see if she remembers this: 'Clap your hands! Stomp your feet! McHenry Trojans can't be beat!' I love you, Mom. I have to stay off this phone. I'll see you in a few months as long as this solar flare doesn't burn us all up or this Ebola doesn't kill all of us. I love you, Mom." She said, "I love you too," and I hung up.

That's when the TV media stopped talking about Ebola vaccines and Ebola all together. The TV started talking and advertising immunity boosters instead of flu vaccines. Sambucol and Tamiflu were the commercials that were on TV at the time. Okay, Sambucol. Are you kidding me? That almost spells my first and last name Sam Cole. And Tamiflu. My wife's name is Tammy.

After that the TV said stay tuned for a presidential announcement. That's when Obama made the announcement about taking a pause. That there would be no more talk about Ebola. Everyone needed to calm down. I felt if he was directly reacting to my phone conversation with my mom. I kept on telling myself that it was all a coincidence, but in my head, it was all too real.

The newscasters at the time were going crazy. I don't know if they were trying this to please me, but it seemed like there were— doing just what I had said to my mom minutes before. This was too weird. A couple of hours later, this one newscast team even dressed up in chicken suits, and one of the broadcasters looked really angry that he had to do a dance in front of the camera. Could they be doing this for me? I wondered. They did look like they were making asses out of themselves. It didn't look like it was their idea that they were dressed that way. Someone had to tell them to do it, which reminded me about what they were doing to those inmates back in the treatment center to get out of prison early. Were they doing this for me? All I knew was the media seemed pissed whatever channel I turned on.

There also had been something on the news about Kenny, the kid I was locked up with in county. He was involved in a high-speed chase, and his face was posted all over the news. Crazy, I was telling one of the guys down there, and he ended up coming out and telling me that he came from that same jail. Then we got to talk about the other inmates whom we worked in the kitchen with who passed away from overdose. We began to share stories and laugh together about the experiences that we went through while being locked up. It was so hard not to mention the whole Officer Holt story, but I managed to keep that one a secret. It was a crazy coincidence that he came from the same jail and the same worker pod that I came from about a year ago.

Poor Kenny, I thought. It looked like he picked up a fifteen-year sentence for that little joyride. In my head, they were telling me something, that they would come after me if I opened my mouth about this to anyone.

CHAPTER 5

Bait and Switch

There was this crazy thing on the local news station down here about a prisoner from this prison in Jacksonville who sold a story to Hollywood about his time in this place for $100,000. He was with some of the officers from here whom I recognized. They were behind him smiling as he held up the check. They were in the conference room, and he looked so happy holding up that check as the guards behind him looked just as happy just to be on TV.

This was too much. It was too much of a coincidence. They must be talking about me. I didn't know if there was some fancy AI system playing a game with me or what. But they were doing this because of me. I knew I wasn't hallucinating from a lack of sleep. They were doing this because of Officer Holt and this story.

That is when I asked one of the guards up in front if I could have a high-ranking officer to come see me so I could see what's going on. When she came, I noticed it was one of the officers all dressed in white. She just so happened to be one of the officers I saw on TV a little while ago. She asked me, "What's wrong with you?" but I could tell behind her eyes she wasn't asking out of concern for my well-being. Her eyes were filled with rage.

I said, "Look, my grandpa was a Chicago cop, and the things that are happening on TV are freaking me out. I have been noticing a lot of innuendoes and coincidences, and these people seem as if they're talking about me."

Her eyes changed when I mentioned *cop*. Then she said, "Come with me, Cole."

So we walked to the infirmary. There I was met by two guards, a nurse, and two plain-clothed guys, all of them seemingly waiting for me to walk in there. One of the plain-clothed men asked, "What's wrong with this guy?" to the officer who brought me in.

She said, "This guy says the TV is out to get him."

I said, "No, that's not what I said. I said that it seems as if someone is listening to my phone conversations, and the media is reacting to what I'm talking about. I don't what to be on TV."

The officer who brought me in asked, "Why do you think you're going to be on TV, Cole?"

"Because I just saw you an hour ago with that kid from here holding a check for a story he wrote."

"That doesn't usually happen here, Cole."

Then I told those people the whole story about Officer Holt and how he committed suicide over the fact that three different types of DNA were found in a dead girl in a prison cell from the county jail I came from. But yeah, I never told anyone besides my psychologist and the warden from the work camp about it.

One of the other officers said, "So you never spoke of this over the phone."

I said no, that I had only spoken of this to the psychologist and the warden.

The other officer in the room who was standing next to him came over and grabbed me by the cheeks. Then he said, "This kid's eyes are dilated. He's on something," as he squeezed my cheeks harder.

I said, "I haven't been taking any drugs in here, so what does that mean?"

Then one of the nurses came up to me and looked into my eyes and said, "His eyes don't look dilated."

"Well, maybe not," the officer said and started to let go of his grip.

He seemed like the guy in charge. He didn't know how to take me when I said that. What I was implying was that maybe someone in there was drugging me. I had left that open for that possibility. He said, "Come with me, Cole." He took me to a private room, stripped me down, and checked to make sure I didn't have anything I wasn't supposed to have. I got redressed, and he put me in a holding cell overnight.

Sleep that night was not an option. I didn't get a wink that night. I was staring up at the ceiling a few hours later when I caught a commotion out of the corner of my eye. There were two security guards looking into my window. As soon as I looked over, I noticed they feared me. The guards jumped up with their eyes wide open. One of the guards yelled a little bit in terror as I turned my head toward them. Then I heard the other guard say, "If you need anything, Cole, you let us know."

"Will do," I said with crackle in my voice. It was kind of funny seeing two huge prison officers get so scared over a guy like me in a prison outfit.

I started to ask God for guidance through all of this and to give me a sign if he was listening. As soon as that thought left my head, he answered me. There was a guy with a baseball cap looking through the window to my cell with the brightest blue eyes. He gave me a nod, looked at my breakfast, looked back at me, gave me a thumbs up, then he walked off. I could swear he spoke to me telepathically and said, "He heard you, good job, and that everything will be okay, Cole." I ran up to the window, but when I looked out the window of my prison door to see who this guy was or where he went, he was gone.

The next morning, they put me in a padded room to talk to another psychologist. When she walked into my cell, I noticed she was with one of the guards from the night before. She asked me if I was okay, and I asked her if she had read the letters I'd been writing. She said yes. Then I told her it's all about numbers and sacrifices that you make for people and that I also believe in the AA program.

She lost her shit. She said, "Ooh, and but you're so young." I didn't know for sure, but it seemed like she was making a threat against me. She never asked me any more questions and walked out. I never saw that lady again.

After the padded room, they sent me to an infirmary bed where there were six or so other guys sitting in their beds. There were two guys who were recently in a fight, each in opposite corners of the room. There was one guy who had a broken leg. The guy with the broken leg asked me what my problem was. I turned to him and shrugged my shoulders without knowing what to tell him. "This place is pretty great," he said to me. "They serve you food in bed and give you double desserts sometimes." By the looks of this kid, that was the last thing he needed. He must have weighed at least four hundred pounds. But I would watch this kid eat as if it were his last meal every night. To me there was something funny about the food. I didn't have any proof, but I just didn't trust it. I limited myself to just two bites every meal.

They had a couple of TVs on in there as well. Now being around the Bible Belt, you know they take their religion seriously. Some Christian speaker was always on. It seemed to me like they were always so pissed about something. I forgot her name. She was an older white lady with big red-lipstick lips. When I was watching her, she was always mad about something. I couldn't tell you what it was. But her face was always about two feet away from the camera. It was as if she was coming out of the TV to get me.

Something in there was telling me to look away from the TV and write. After recently reading about all the different ancient religions, I was going to put it in a way that to me seemed like it was a lot easier to understand. So I wrote a letter to my mom. I needed to thank her anyway and let her know I was okay.

> Dear Mom, I'm doing good. I'm staying off
> the phone for a while. I'll see you when I get out.
> I've been reading in here. What do you think of
> this concept I thought of?
> Mind: Pythagoras—the only just thing is to
> sacrifice for people, theory of everything, a lover
> of learning, stay being the student never the wise
> man, and #

Heart: Jesus—daily reflection, daily reprieve and forgiveness, the way to reason, and to listen for answers

Gut: Budda—work, meditation, freedom of breathing, enjoying the silence of everything.

I'm sure there was more to that letter. I just don't remember.

That's when I felt these cosmic beats that were surrounding me at that time. I felt like I was losing it. "Ta ta tee tee ta," my old music teacher in grade school used to say. It was a way to teach us how to create a song. It was a beat like that. Maybe more like an Indian drum beat that I could almost anticipate before the next beat. Or maybe it was just all in my head. But I must have looked like I was going crazy using my hands, waving them around like a conductor would be standing in front of a symphony or an orchestra.

After that, the next day they sent me to go see another psychologist. He was this guy who looked like your typical psychologist, very distinguished with balding hair and reading glasses that were falling off his nose. I sat down in his office. I had never seen him before. He introduced himself to me and asked me to have a seat in the chair opposite his. "So, Cole, you don't mind if I call you that, do you? Or would you like for me to call you Samuel?"

"Cole is fine," I said to him. He asked me if there was anything bothering me. I said, "No. Well, I do have a problem with what's going on in that treatment center of yours. What those counselors are doing to those men in there is something I have never seen before in my life."

He nodded his head and said, "Yeah, but what about anything else?"

I said, "I might be hallucinating from the lack of sleep. I have only been getting two to three hours a night since I got in here."

"Yeah, so I hear you have an alcohol problem on the outside."

"Yeah, that I did and that I was drinking so much I was masking my emotions."

"Masking your emotions. So that's it?"

"Yep."

That seemed to piss him off because when I left, I could hear him swearing at himself. Even one of the guards said that he'd never seen him have that kind of reaction before. Then the guard asked me what I had said to him, I just shrugged my shoulders and said, "I don't know." He stormed out of his office and slammed the exit door behind him.

The next day they sent me to a meditation meeting in a group setting where they had this crazy-looking lady ringing this little bell with incense smoke going around her. She would ring a couple of times then chant. All the other guys were getting into it, so I tried not to laugh.

Then I asked if she had ever heard of Ram Dass and how breathing techniques will calm people. I told her you must focus by breathing deeply all the way in through the nose, then letting it out slowly through the mouth and to focus and stare at one small spot in the room, which can give you a good sense of being and maybe even free your mind from the negativity that surrounds it sometimes.

Then I talked about all these coincidences and cosmic beats. She said, "Interesting." Then I mentioned Pythagoras and how it is all about sacrifices you make for other people.

Then she said to me, "Isn't it cool to find a book at exactly the right time and in exactly the right place that you need to read it?" like she knew what was happening to me, which she probably did. I didn't say anything after that. We left, and I started to talk to one of the guys about it. Then he began to talk about his beliefs and that he didn't believe in coincidences. And I began to say, "Yeah, everything is relative, and everything is connected."

After that, we played some chess together when we got back to our room. I felt kind of embarrassed in front of the other guys when they were making fun of me, repeating what I said. They yelled out, "Hey, Cole" and breathed deeply like they were having sex. I stopped talking about it after that and lay down to try to get some sleep.

The next morning, I sent that letter about Pythagoras to my mom. It was just so weird when I came back to my bunk after sending the letter, there was an ADT commercial on where there was a protective ring going around the world, like the TV was telling me something. Like somehow sending that letter would set off a chain reaction that would maybe save the world somehow. Crazy, right? I still hadn't been getting enough sleep. But I swear the TV was flipping out and acting like it was possessed. I swear it was because of me, of how I was holding the media hostage down here in a way.

The media would be making fun of me too, putting pregnant women on and then have them do Limone's training, which was like what I was talking about when I said to that meditation lady how I used meditation to calm myself and other people down here. *They must have cameras all over this place*, I thought.

Then came a news broadcast on St. Louis. It was showing the ark that they have over there. That ark in my head started to hold some significance to my situation. I told my cellie about it and said, "That ark being in St. Louis seemed to represent to me as if it were bridging the gap, connecting the differences between sinner and saint." He looked at me with some crazy eyes and didn't have a response to what I said.

After getting my normal two-hour sleep, the next day, I got the slip that they were going to send me to my original psychologist. I walked in and had a seat in one of her chairs. I said, "It's been a month. Why haven't you come for me and asked me how I was doing"?

She said, "Sorry, Cole, I was busy." Then she asked me with a tremble in her voice, "Why didn't you open up and tell that psychiatrist the other day about Officer Holt?"

"I didn't want to spread any rumors that the reason Officer Holt did it was because of his family. As long as you don't spread any rumors about me."

"About you?"

"Yeah, you know that if your name is Samuel and if you're reading the Bible for the first time. It kind of messes with your head. The similarities in there…"

"What kind of similarities?"

"You know I kind of treat my girlfriend as a friend. You know that it kind of sounds similar. Like they're talking about me."

As I was speaking, I could see her hand shaking as she was writing down everything I said with a smile on her face. I was speaking fast on purpose. But I believe she was keeping up with what I said. Then she asked me, "Are you sure you're not crazy, Cole? What does your wife say about you?"

"I don't know. She doesn't think that I'm any crazier than anyone else is."

"So that's it?"

"Yep, that's it."

She smiled with satisfaction as I left. But she missed something. Little did she know what the true meaning of the word *family* meant when I said it. She didn't ask, and I didn't tell.

The next day I woke up and went into the rec room with the other early risers and started to watch the news. At the time there were only three news stations on, and all of them seemed as if they were trying to rile us up for a fight. I could feel the rage on the TV when I was there. That's when the ruling came back that they were not to indict the cop who shot Michael Brown as they let him go right in the face of all the angry protesters. But I could tell it wasn't only about Michael Brown anymore. It was everything that the establishment had been shoveling down our throats for the last couple of years. There was so much rage coming out of that screen. I could tell that they wanted me out of the way so they could have their war. And at the time, they thought I was.

That's when they sent me back to the psychologist. It was a long walk over there. I sprained my ankle jumping off the top bunk the night before. I was limping all the way across the courtyard to her office. Anyway, I got in there and she asked, "Are you okay?"

I said, "Yep" with a smile on my face.

"How's that ankle?"

"Fine."

"Well, do you have anything to add?"

I said, "Nope" with a smile on my face.

She said, "Well, have a nice Thanksgiving."

"Yeah, you know what, you too." Then I left. I bet she thought I was going to be upset by what was going on or maybe even start to get scared and bawl like I did before. But I didn't. I kept my cool. With me being so calm and happy, that's when they probably looked at my transcripts and read what I had said about the reason Officer Holt committed suicide. It was because of his family. The reason wasn't because of his blood family, but it was because of the whole unified policing community and establishment.

When I got back to my bunk, that's when all hell broke loose. The protesters on TV were going nuts, and the cops weren't doing anything to stop them. I wondered if I had something to do with all of this. All these guards were rushing in and out of my room, giving me the most insanely raging looks. Going through all my stuff, taking whatever papers that they could find with my writing on it. Moving me around from one pod to another. They were going through everyone else's stuff too. One of the guards even pointed at the TV and gave me a head nod as he stared me down as if to say I caused this. One of them held one arm to the side and one arm into the air like Superman did in those old movies as he passed my room.

As I was watching the protesters riot, I was surprised to see all the white people rioting with them, which led me to think I really don't believe that all of this was even about Michael Brown and police brutality on black people. It was about fear. Fear of the system that had this control over them for so long. Maybe a fractured system that was not giving its people a voice anymore. I was feeling the anger they felt against these elites. Basically, they were telling us we were going to do what they told us to do even after what they did after the banking system failed them in the '08 banking bailout crisis. This riot had been building up in America for a long time. America was looking for a change in the system. I think people were upset when they thought Obama was going to give it to them, but he ended up turning the system even more against us than ever.

I finally started to catch on what I was here to do. I wasn't here to start a civil war. I was here to stop one. I played them good too with that story hook, line and sinker. There would be no way now they would give the order to strike back against the protesters who were attacking the police after what they knew about Officer Holt and what he wrote in his suicide letter. It was because of his family that he committed suicide. The family of his whole unified policing community. And now they knew what he truly meant when he wrote that. Just as the riot started and after I got back to my bunk and looked at what I had created, it left me scared, but I stood firm. I could not show it.

See, I believe CNN wanted this war to happen. This media and these elites, I think planned this whole thing but failed when they started to listen to me because most likely they thought maybe this story when I came out with it was going to push people over the top and start fighting each other. But little did they know what kind of impact a guy sitting in this prison cell could have to turn this whole thing around like that. I would joke in front of the TV with the other inmates saying that I threw a wrench in the wheels of time. At the time I felt that I was right.

Obama even came on the screen and said it wasn't right for the police to do nothing and that the police needed to start fighting back against the protesters. It was almost like he wanted the war too with the democrats behind him. It would make sense with all the failures he had while he was president. I couldn't say for sure. It did seem that way, though. The rioters and the protesters went on and on. It started to spread to Lost Angeles, New York, and Chicago.

It seemed to weaken off in Chicago, though. Thank God. I didn't want to worry about my baby girl up there. I swear if anything happened to her and I wasn't there to protect her because I didn't want to fry like bacon for these people, I would have flipped out for sure, maybe even hurt someone in there.

CHAPTER 6

Singular Consciousness

All these movies were coming out around this time, and it was almost as if they were coinciding with what was going on in real life. Like that *The Hunger Games: Mockingjay* movie previews. It showed Jennifer Lawrence yelling onto the screen. It was almost as if she was coming out of the screen as I was watching her. "I have a message for president Snow. If we burn…then you're going to burn with us!" This still makes my eyes water up today. I felt she was speaking for me to President Obama at the time. When all these protesters were freaking out about Michael Brown, Ebola, racial injustice, that solar flare, the space quake, there was a lot of justified madness going on at the time. I felt the only thing holding these all together was me. The militarized police at the time with their tactical gear reminded me of the movie *Soylent Green*. I was really surprised that they didn't make the decision to send the troops to the protesters and declare martial law, but they never did. It did feel like it was because of me and this story.

But yeah, these movies and movie previews at the time were predicting things that were happening in real life it, like *Planet of the Apes*, which was set in a post-pandemic country where the apes were fighting the humans. Or the movie *The Dark Knight Rises* or the movie *Selfless*. Those movie previews looked like what was going on out there in real life. It was movie preview after preview.

When they came out with a movie mocking North Korea and Kim Jong Un when President Obama was planning a trip over there, it started to seem as though it had become too much of a coincidence even for President Obama. He launched an investigation. He said he was going to give a $5 million award to the person who could tell him what was going on with the movies. Right after he made that announcement, I got the slip to see the psychiatrist again.

When I got over there, it was your typical small talk, trying to feel me out. I knew what I had to do. I politely played dumb and made chitchat with her. With a smile on my face before I walked out the door, I said, "Have a nice day."

When I got back to the TV in the rec room, Obama said the $5 million reward was off. Then he called it the Sony Pictures hack. I think they said a group called the Lazarus Group was behind it all, "supposably." But I believe there were some true, unexplainable miracles happening there that to this day I can't explain.

But I don't know; the timing was just too perfect. It was the unified creative source of information being downloaded to all these artists and writers at the time to save us from what was going on in real life. But, I don't know, maybe they wanted us to fight too. It was hard to tell, but I know it did want me. I could feel it. Telepathically I could even hear it.

There was a lot of things that they were showing us that pissed me off as well like the last episode of *Sons of Anarchy* where the main characters were all locked away in a prison cell, having butt sex with each other and the other inmates in the end. Gross. That was my favorite show. Why did it have to end like that? Nothing against gay people or anything, but these guys were straight as could be.

I felt that this thing wanted me. It was coming right out of the TV down there. Whatever higher or lower power that was out there, he was pissed. I never experienced that level of intimidation before. It had be some sort of supernatural force behind it all. It scared me to death. It was so hard to keep my cool and not freak out. My thoughts seemed to become a transmitter to it and for whoever or whatever was attacking our country. I felt as if they were speaking through me into my thoughts. There was spiritual warfare going on, and I was winning from what I could tell. The higher power out there didn't seem to like it. The TV was possessed, and it was mad that I played a trick on him or her, whoever was running the show. I was ruining their plan for us to go into civil war.

I had to stop watching this TV for a while. So I dove into writing Tammy and baby Olivia. I wrote a lot of letters down there to Tammy at least once a week. I always finished each letter with XOXOs, which meant hugs and kisses. I hadn't used this way of writing since I was in grade school. But ever since I was locked up, I'd been using them in my letters. It did bring me back to the days of writing to my different girlfriends back in the day in junior high. But anyway, a new song came on a music station down there called "Ex's & Oh's" by Ellie King. I'd never heard that song before, but man, if you have ever listened to the lyrics of that song…I have to say the x's and o's did haunt me. Like the creative cosmic force was trying to push me off my rocker and freak out. Believe me, it was working; but there was no way I could show it. I was almost home.

There would be little slips I would find that would just appear out of nowhere too, telling me what to do. But I knew at the time whatever I would have said would have made the situation a lot worse out there. So I thought the best thing to do was just stay quiet and let them be the ones who would go crazy with worry of what kind of trouble I could have made for them if I spoke out about this to anyone. My temperature was rising, and I was getting angry and maybe a little crazy.

There was something in the music too. Another example, "Uptown Funk," a song sung by Mark Ronson, came on TV for the first time; and I could swear when he sang those lyrics, "too hot, hot dam," he was actually singing, "too hot, hot Sam" when I first heard it. The music that was coming out at the time, I felt, was being directed to me and this whole situation that I was in.

I was going to lose it when there was a new movie preview that came on called *Tammy*. Are you serious? That movie got me so mad when I saw the preview for the first time. Calm down, Sam. It's just a stupid movie. It had this overweight actress Melissa McCarthy. She was playing kind of a poor Midwestern woman. It seemed to me at the time that they were making fun of my wife Tammy. The actress was all loud, talking as if she was a trucker.

There was no way I was going to flip out. There was no way to prove it. How could I when I was stuck in there? I tried to make excuses and tried to tell myself that this was just all a big coincidence. But one coincidence after another, they started to add up. These movies were thought up most likely years ago. How were these movies pushing me the way they were? That kind of magic seems so impossible to believe even as I'm writing this now. But if you look all of this up, it was the timing of all this. That it was happening was even harder to believe.

I started to get brave enough to talk to the guys around this time in front of the TV camera, knowing now that I was being watched and recorded through that TV. I turned to my fellow black inmates and asked them, "Are you the way you are because the TV tells you who you are, or is it because you tell yourself who you are?"

Then I would turn the channel, and I would see Miley Cyrus on a wrecking ball, naked, singing her song. I was telling the guys about it, saying, "What's the deal with her? She used to be such a nice girl. Hopefully, no little girls were looking up to her growing up as a kid." Then with some anger, I held my hand to my mouth to call out to those Hollywood elites. "Show me your tits!" I yelled out. "Basically, that's what actors and actresses are. They're meant for entertainment purposes only. They should not be people we look up to. They are there for our entertainment purposes only," I said to the guys. Our leaders should be the people we voted into office. The congressmen and women whom I voted at the time had no idea who they were with the lack of knowledge we were getting from that stupid TV at the time.

Then after that, I started jokingly talking to the TV, and the black inmates who stood around me talked about BET too—the Black Entertainment Television. I asked these guys how they would feel if there was a WET channel, White Entertainment Television. I just felt the hate that was coming out of that TV whenever that channel was on. It was hard to ignore when you would see all these inmates all riled up every time that channel was on. In my opinion, it was gaslighting them as well for a fight.

I just remember saying how networks like these separate and segregate us more than they bring us all together. I started to stick my chest out in a way black people do sometimes when they are confronted by cops, then waving my hands around, I said, "What's the matter with you? Do you maybe get some BET in you?" Then with a paranoid look on my face, I looked around like I was high on crack. Then I said with one finger over my lips, "Shh, I'm hunting wabbits" like Elmer Fudd did in those funny old Bugs Bunny cartoons.

The guys didn't catch on to that one. They just looked at me, nodded, and smiled at me. The message was meant to be for the people who were spying on me anyway. I think I made my point. I could almost feel them watching me, and I was picturing the faces that they were making when I said what I had said.

I knew it was bad for people who were doing this, having a baby with multiple women. But that was the way the welfare system worked. It encourages you to be a single mother so the family household gets more money when the family breaks up. Black families in the 1920s and 30s stayed together more so than white people did. It wasn't until the civil rights movement that, that group of people went in a different direction. Back in the twenties when segregation was going on, they were building their own colleges, their own churches. It wasn't until the democrats sold them on these reparations package that they started to feel inferior, in my opinion. That free money can turn evil if there are stipulations that go along with it. Believe me, I know from experience.

Some people were doing it on purpose. Maybe I was watching too much Jerry Spinger at the time, watching everyone there getting all upset over who the baby's father was. I always thought that poor kid when he grew up, having to watch a recording of his parents arguing who was going to take care of him, his father denying him on television, he would be thinking as if he were some sort of a burden to his parents. He then would be wondering why he was ever born. People would be laughing and getting all happy when that DNA test came back and the result of the test wasn't what they expected.

Dancing, laughing all around while the mother got all upset and crying.

It made me sad thinking about it. Kids between the ages of one and seven are like programming on a computer. If the program is messed up, you're going to have a nonfunctioning computer. I believe that works with humans as well. I myself have two illegitimate kids out there, and I feel guilty as hell about it, not being a part of the kids' life and them growing up without any kind of father to speak of. It's just too easy to accidently get a girl pregnant. I was only with this girl one time, and she ended up keeping the kid. See, that's the thing. Women have choices; men have responsibilities. She never wanted anything from me. I still feel guilty though It's human nature. When I kept seeing black inmate after black inmate being proud and bragging on how many kids they had with multiple different women with no way to support them, I knew I was dealing with a different kind of monster completely.

In the early nineteen hundreds, I hear the white population in the south were doing the same thing—having multiple children with no way of being able to support them. But they stayed together for the most part. I think they were mostly doing it to turn their kids into cheap labor, but that's a different story. They weren't having kids so they would be a cash cow for any kind of welfare system. I don't know what kind of welfare was given to mothers in the early twentieth century, but I'm sure it was something. So white people did it too. They were just more monogamist about it. The biggest thing was religion telling us to do so, that wearing protection was a sin. We all had to be fruitful and multiply. This never made much sense to me.

Around this time Pope Francis became the new pope. When I was watching him talk, I could see he was more up-front and honest than any other pope had been. He really didn't seem to be too scared to talk about the true issues that plagued this world like popes in the past did. I was watching him stepping on the world stage for the first time. He went on to say that he knew there had been problems in the past on the issue of child molestation in the church, and how he would make sure that it would never happen again, and that there would be more transparency in the church.

Then he went on to say that as a society, we were never to meant to breed like rabbits. Holy shit. He said it. That was always one of my biggest problems with the church I had—the scripture that read "be fruitful and multiply and replenish the earth," with no birth control, no other reason to have sex than to multiply; and it is the only way. That may have worked two thousand years ago. You would think they would have come up with a more up-to-date version by now with the world population as big as it is.

It is that way of thinking that annoyed me. Religion never talked about the condition of the planet. Because if you believe in Jesus, he will be coming down soon to rescue all of us in the rapture. So you'd better just keep on doing what you're doing. Just believe in him so we can live for eternity in heaven someday.

Telling people not to wear protection when having sex even if you can't afford to have children—that just seems so wrong to me. To some people, I guess, they see it as a way to get another paycheck.

It seemed like they were all bragging about how many kids they had down here. Ten kids. Fifteen kids. Nobody in there seemed to have less than three baby mommas. It just made me sick. They were all proud of it like it was a good thing. Because with every kid that they have out there, the more money would be sent to them in prison. Did you know prisoners' children's moms get money for every day that they would be in prison? And it wasn't just the black guys who were doing this. It was the white guys too. It was a mad dash every day for the phones to see how much money they could squeeze out of their baby mommas for commissary money to buy all their snacks and extra clothing that they would get.

The prison system had no complaints; they were making money hand over fist. Why go against what the church was telling them to do?

But yeah, the pope said that. We should not be breeding like rabbits. Funny, it was just the other day that I was talked to a guy about it in front of the TV. It did seem like I had something to do with what the pope had just said. It could have been a coincidence, but with all these coincidences adding up, it was hard to keep making excuses that all of this was all in my head.

The riots got stronger. ISIS, a new religion that was based off an ancient one, was going strong and started to go after the Taliban. Obama thought this might be a good thing until they started publicly cutting off people's heads, then destroying all the ancient relics over there. I bet he was thinking of that old saying "The enemy of my enemy is my friend," but they ended up being extremely more violent than he probably ever expected, so I bet he had to eat his words on that one.

A couple of days later, they sent me back to the psychologist. I sat down, and I said nothing. It was almost like a contest on who would speak first. So out of boredom, I said, "I'm just here to answer any questions that you may have for me."

She said, "Okay, so you're good,"

"Yep."

"So you don't have any more problems, Cole?"

"Nope. You know, if I don't like it here, then maybe I shouldn't come back."

"Right. Well—"

Before she could finish, I said, "What I saw when I first came in here was a war. Instead, what I see now is everyone coming together in peace."

"It all turned out better than you expected," she said.

"Yes, it did!"

Then she stood up, trying to rush me out of the door before I could say anything else. Then I left, trying not to say anything else for fear of being put into a mental hospital or turning things from bad to worse out there. So I did the only smart thing I could do. I shut up and left.

When I came back to the rec room, I saw on TV riots and protests going on in every major city in America. It seemed the people in France were going crazy over there too. The whole *Charlie Hebdo* thing was going on in the streets, and they were filled with people wall to wall. I'd never seen so many people all going crazy all over the world at once. I'd never seen this planet so enraged. It seemed as if the whole world was on fire.

If you don't remember, the *Charlie Hebdo* shooting was where a group of terrorists went in and killed three or four cartoonists in the building because of what they drew. They drew their Prophet Muhammad as a cartoon doing something silly in one of their newspapers over there. So some terrorists broke in and killed them. It seemed the people were losing their minds based on what I saw over the news, their hands up in the air, yelling to the camera. They had these ambulances with SAMU77 on them. *Come on*, I thought. *That's my name and the year I was born with a U in the middle like I caused this or something.* But yeah, those SAMU77s were all over the news that day as well.

Then came another commercial for Sambucol and Tamiflu, the medications they were advertising for Ebola. After that another preview came on for the movie *Mockingjay*. That girl got good close-up in that movie preview when she yelled, "I got a message for you, President Snow. If we're going to burn…then you're going to burn with us."

"I got to lay down," I said out loud to myself. The voices in my head were in full effect. It was telling me that this was all my fault. And the TV was calling me out, but with the lack of sleep I was getting, I had to try to convince myself that it was all from the lack of sleep, and I was just hallucinating all of this. Or maybe it was all just a coincidence. I wish it was all just a bad dream. This had to be all in my head. When I got back to my bunk, I put earplugs in and a sock tied around my eyes, saying half-jokingly with tears rolling down my face, "There's no place like home. There's no place like home. Stay strong, Sam. Be confident. You must make it through this. Just keep quiet and keep smiling and play stupid." But it had been so long since I got to do that before I heard the call "chow time" one of the guards yelled into our wing.

I always had somewhere to watch TV, though, so there was no way to escape from the madness I was feeling. There were the nineteen TVs in my room and the two TVs in the rec room. There was a new movie preview on as I was walking out the door for lunch, dinner, or breakfast. This movie preview was called *Unbroken*. It was about an airplane bomber from World War II. His name was Louis Zamperini, which kind of sounded a lot like my mother's maiden name, Zapparato. It gave me some inspiration being stuck in there. It had this kid Zamperini holding up a large log up, crying out in front of the camera in a Japan prison camp, yelling and sweating, looking really skinny. He was letting out a war cry as if to say he wasn't going to let the warden get the best of him, which kind of reminded me of my situation here.

In one of the scenes from *Unbroken*, Louie got yelled at by his brother in the stands while he was running in an Olympic race. "Go get 'em, you dumb dago." That damn TV was pushing me. I knew it was, what with me being Italian. It was almost as if the TV knew the exact time I was looking at it. I felt like it was alive, watching me and making me look at it just when it wanted to. It wanted me to come out with this story so they would have their great reset. But there was no way I could live with myself if this country went into some sort of civil war or race war over me and what I said. I knew what I had to do was just sit back and take this craziness for a little while longer.

At least there was the cafeteria. It gave me a break from being in that dorm and in that rec room. When I went to the cafeteria, I watched these people eating their food. They looked like they were dazed and confused about what was going on with the TVs as I was. This one guy came up to me and said, "Have you been watching TV?" I said yes, and we were both wide-eyed for a second as we looked at each other. "What the hell is going on?" he asked me as we were standing in line to get our food. He asked me if I was seeing the same things as he saw. He said that it was like the TV was possessed or something. I was just glad I was not the only one, I told him.

At least the food was good—beef stir-fry, fried chicken, spaghetti. It did seem like no matter what they gave us to eat, there was always somebody complaining about it. "This food is bogus," they would say. They seemed to use that term a lot in there. You're bogus for doing this or that, as if they felt wronged by somebody. It was a term I just never used before. I thought that it just meant fake. But the food being so good meant I had to spend less on commissary. My aunt Lori gave me $200 on my books, which meant I could order a candy bar or two. I could also buy my tea. I drank a lot of tea there. It seemed to calm me down. Coffee made me more riled up. Coffee is good when you have work, but when you're just sitting around, it leaves a void of excessive energy.

I was thinking I would give a thank-you note to Aunt Lori after lunch. When I got back to my wing, I noticed this guy selling these cards that he drew up and colored himself. The card had Winnie the Poo on it as well as other characters. It was drawn very well, and I was impressed by his artwork. The title read, "The reasons why I love you," which was kind of creepy, but I bought it off him anyway with a summer sausage and ramen noodles. This note signified what God felt for humanity at the time rather than a thank-you note for my aunt. But it read, "Number 1 reason, you're smart; number 2, you're angelic; number three, you're punctual. Then it read, "Oops, looks like I ran out of space," with it being all the space it had on that card. After I sent that letter out to my aunt a couple of hours later, it did seem, when I turned on the news that night, they were reacting to what I had written through an interview with one of the newscasters who were crying on TV that night. But I couldn't tell for sure.

CHAPTER 7

Family Visit

My birthday came up on November 2; I was thirty-seven. My family was all writing me letters, wishing me a happy birthday. It was nice of them considering how much longer it takes to write a letter. I was getting a lot of support with letters from family, even my distant family, which made me feel good and guilty at the same time. I was starting to question if I should have just shut up and just did what they told me to do. I would have been back with my daughter by now. I couldn't take it back now, though.

Maybe a week or two after my birthday, a guard said to me as I was walking in from the yard, "Cole, you had better call your mother."

I was thinking, *Why is a guard telling me this?* Afraid of what I might say over the phone, I said, "I'm good. I'll see her when I get out."

Then the other guard started to laugh and said, "Mommy wants to talk to you."

The antagonizing guards that they have working in there were intense. I swear that there must be some kind of special training before they hire you for this position just to make sure you're an asshole first above anything else. They were good; they almost made me feel guilty enough to do it. But I knew better. I wanted my last recorded phone message to be left alone. What I had said when I said it was perfect. I knew that would be some sort of proof for my future self. What I went through in this place really happened. And all this that I was experiencing wasn't some sort of dream. I wish I had that recording now. I wonder if they kept all my phone conversations and recordings after all these years.

Anyway, I didn't want my mom to drive all the way down here from McHenry. I was sure she was worried sick about me. I knew she was getting a little freaked out about the fact that I was not calling her. Her constant paranoia over her kids was intense. I would always make a joke, saying, "At least I'm not dead in a ditch somewhere." I felt bad, but it needed to be done. I couldn't call her.

I might have accidentally told her something. I thought that might put her in harm's way, which in my mind at the time would lead to her or my family members falling victim to some kind of covenant accident. If you know what I mean. I had no trust in the government. Hell, I still don't!

The next day after lunch, an officer came to our wing, which was kind of unusual. They usually didn't show up unless there was a fight or something serious. But no, she was asking for me. I could see her pointing at me, and I read her lips as she said "Cole" through the plexiglass window.

"Cole, you have a visitor," one of the guards yelled in my wing.

"Damn, bud, I'm right here," I said to him, standing two feet away. It wasn't a visiting day, I thought. Then I asked her who was visiting me. I didn't write out a request form.

"Come with me, Cole," the officer said. While ignoring my last question, she led me outside. I didn't want to cause any more trouble than I already have, so I followed her. Well, at least they were going to give me an opportunity to speak with her. I think they wanted to see for themselves what I would say to her.

I was waiting to be let into the visitor's lodge outside when I saw the warden for the first time. And I thought I was tall. This guy had to be at least six feet, ten inches. Good looking guy, kind of on the skinny side, he was black; and he was walking right to me with three other plain-clothed people on each side. The warden kind of looked at me as if he feared me. Two of the other ones stared at me with concern; the other four ignored me and pretended I wasn't there. I pretended not to notice and gave him a nod with my head held high like a soldier would. He seemed to be walking into a side door behind the room I was walking into. I couldn't tell you for sure, but to me it sure looked as if it was the monitoring room. They were going to have cameras in there when I talked to my mom. I knew it. There was no way they we're going to put me in a special room to visit my mom on a day that wasn't even visiting day. And I didn't even give them a request form. These people love their rules here. When they break one of them, it's a big deal in there. All those people were going to be watching and listening to my every word.

So after I stripped and they patted me down, they walked me down the hall where my mom sat in this big room alone with one guard at his desk.

"Hi, Mom," I said.

"Hello, Sam," she said as we immediately hugged each other.

"Stop, Mom, don't cry. I'm fine. What are you doing here? I told you that I was done with that phone in here, that I would see you when I got out."

"I'm worried about you."

"Mom, I'm fine. I'll be out in a couple of months. Well anyway, how's everything going with everyone?"

"Good. Scott (my brother) and Shelly (his wife) just had their baby."

"What's her name?"

"Sadie. Why?"

"They are still living in our old 316 house?"

"Yeah, they're doing good over there. And get this, she was born a day after your birthday on November 3."

"And her name is Sadie?"

"Yeah, why?"

"Okay. I'm only saying this because I don't think I'm being recorded. Mom, do you remember *Bogus's Normal Day?*"

"The book you wrote in the sixth grade?"

"Yeah. Do you remember it was about an alien kid from Pluto who wanted to get his cheek pierced, but his mom wouldn't let him do it? So then, he gave his mom mind control capsules to turn his uptight mom into a cool one. Then he took her to a concert the next day and not only did Bungas wake up with his cheek pierced, but the mom did too. Then when she looked in the mirror, she let out a long scream."

"Yeah, I remember."

"Well, everyone in here is calling each other bogus. 'You're bogus.' 'This food is bogus.' I'm Bogus, and this is my normal day."

"I thought the alien's name was Bungas. Bogus means fake," she said as if to say that I wasn't fake.

"Yeah, you're right, but I was so close," I said. "Just like all these other names in here. Even these movies that are coming out. They're so close. It's as if someone is trying to tell me something in here. They have this movie coming out called *Unbroken*, where the main character is named Zamperini, which sounds a lot like Zapparato, Mom. It seems like an inspirational movie. You should check it out." Then I asked, "What street was I born on? Was it Bay Road?"

"No, it was Monroe. Why?"

"There's something about Bay on the Bay. I don't know." But I was born on Mon…roe. It reminds me of the Monroe Institute where they explore the conscious and the unconscious mind." She wouldn't have known what I was talking about, so I switched subjects. Hey, Mom, your new house is on Brown Street, right?"

"Yes."

Like Michael Brown, I thought. "See, Mom, all about these connections. All of this can't be just all a coincidence. It's all about these connections, and I was meant to be here." I sat up in my chair as she looked around for something or someone for help. In my mind she was looking for a hidden camera for someone to help her. "This is my fight. Don't worry about me," I said.

"You might want to watch what you say around here, Sam." It wasn't concern that was behind her eyes; it started to turn into fear. She was afraid for me.

Then I started singing a Bob Dylan tune. "How many roads must a man walk down before you call him a man?" Then I said, "There's something about the streets that I've lived on, Mom. It's all connected. It's all about these connections. I saw the map, Mom."

"Map?" she asked.

"You know, I found this book in here with a funny-looking cross, and it has an ancient map of where they said the one would come from. This map is in a Knights Templar book where they explain all the world's ancient religions. This map has a road called Chapel Hill Road winding down to a road called North. Then it showed going up two blocks into three houses. That looks a lot like our McHenry house. That's our house! The 316 house, isn't it?"

"Right," she said as if she had seen the map before herself. "I bet you won't be going back to drinking when you get out of here, will you, Sam?"

Wow, she saw the map too, I thought to myself. "Have you ever heard of a Jacob's Ladder?" I said.

"Yeah, why?"

"Well, each rung of the ladder gets harder and harder to climb. All I know is it's going to hurt bad when I fall. As I started getting up, I said to her, "I'm fine that this is my fight, that each day I spend in here just seems to be a little bit longer and harder than the last. I'll see you in a couple of months. Don't worry about me, Mom. I just can't know about anything bad going on out there. If I find out something happened to Olivia and I wasn't there to protect her because I didn't want to go through their stupid little program, do you have any idea how mad I'd be?"

"I can kind of see that," she said.

I gave her a hug, and I said, "Thank you, Mom."

"Thank me. Thank me for what!"

"For looking out for Olivia."

"Oh, she's a pleasure." I gave her a hug, then I walked away.

Now the guard was watching us and was overhearing our conversation. He took me to the changing room where I could see his hands were shaking as he was patting me down. I could tell in his eyes that he was scared too. He didn't say anything to me as we walked back to my pod. He just was shaking his head—I believe in disbelief—the whole way back.

"Okay, here's your prisoner," he said to the security guard at the front desk. He turned to me with this rage and hate behind his eyes and told me to go back to my bunk. So I went back to my bunk and put some headphones on from a radio that one of the other inmates gave me before he left.

There were a lot of religious channels down here. I was given a radio a couple of weeks from a guy who had been released. I'd been listening to a few of them for a while now, and I could swear they all knew all about my situation after I let those Jehovah's Witness preachers have it months prior. One of them was a preacher named John Hagee. Well, he started talking about God and that the only way to reach him is through Jesus with all your heart. It was kind of the way I was describing it through my letter.

Then he started to read scripture, something about a man to protect against God's wrath. Then he started to cry. That's when Hagee started to talk about this man who would be giving us an olive tree branch and how it was a sign from God. He was watching me in there, talking to my mom. He had to be. Then he started to cry over the radio I was listening to. That's when I started to cry a little bit too, knowing now how deep this rabbit hole had gotten.

When I looked up the meaning of Olivia, the book said it meant "peace and victory," which in my mind's eye seemed to be the most appropriate name my wife could have named our daughter. I knew the preachers were watching every move I made and most likely had some sort of listening device in my bunk as well. There were too many coincidences with the words that I spoke to the guys and what I was listening to on these radio stations that it seemed to match up perfectly to what I had said.

See, I didn't even think about that when I thanked my mom for looking after Olivia. They were the ones who made that connection to the olive tree. Then they were trying to call me a gift from God of some sort. And this other woman was calling me a lord of some sort. Then she was talking over the radio about what would happen if there were demigods on this planet. Then she said that she could see how other people would be envious if I were to come out as they called me a gift.

Then Hagee came back on. He started talking about the tabernacle and a lot of other prophecies. Then he mentioned what you do when everything out there is pushing you to come out into the open and be recognized to the world, and there's something inside of you telling you to hold back, not yet. That's when he started to talk about the pause that was predicted in the Bible. He went on and on. I wish I had recordings of them all.

He also talked about an old prediction that the Son of God would be carried down a hill by an ass or a donkey. Nobody knew what that meant at the time of Christ. But that's how Jesus was recognized by the church as the Son of God. Jesus rode a donkey down from a hill, and he was recognized as the Son of God by the priest at the time. They got to talk about the tabernacle, and what that meant was interesting stuff. He was a witness to these miracles, but for me, I was still trying to write these all off on chance. How could I be anything else than who I am? I'm nobody special. They couldn't be talking about me.

It would get old listening to him talking after a while, and I would go back to talking with the guys. I was still upset on how my brother-in-law Denise died last year of a fentanyl overdose. I would talk to these guys about staying away from pharmaceuticals, that those are the type of drugs that will kill you, and that that it didn't make much sense that some of them were serving these long sentences for coke when it very rarely kills anyone. "You guys ever try mushrooms? That is the way to go," I said. All you need is a little bit, and it doesn't turn you into a fiend."

Knowing that there had to be some sort of listening device in there, I had to find a way to get these preachers off my back. I started talking to this obese black man. His name was Anthony Hill, and everyone just called him Ant. "So your name is Ant Hill," I said. "Funny, you kind of look like a huge anthill.

"Very funny. Who told you my last name was Hill?"

"I saw it on your name tag at lunch."

"Your name is Samuel Cole. Kind of sounds like a gun."

I said yeah, that I was one letter off. There was an old civil war gun named Samuel Colt back in the day. I said, "Instead of a gun, I was just a lump of coal. Just a lump of coal that you might find in your Christmas stocking if you were bad that year."

Now being so close to Christmas and all, I got a laugh from the guys. "Did you just say that you were a lump of coal, Cole?" Yep, a lump of coal. It was a way of getting back at the preachers to stay away from calling me a gift of any sort. I had to play this game just in case this wasn't all in my head.

Then I started telling the guys about the first night that I got here. I woke everyone up in the room I was in from a dream I had. I dreamt I was on an airplane and I was stopping a terrorist from blowing up the plane. I woke up yelling, "It's a bomb! It's a bomb!" I asked, "Am I the bomb?"

"Damn, Cole, what do you mean by that?"

I didn't say anything after that. I just let that conversation go silent and started talking about something else. But that led me to think about Obama's name too—*O* meaning protection and *bomb* meaning me. Or maybe even to keep his hands off the button. I don't know. Then I thought of his middle name; that's just insane.

I felt such hostility and anger from the media around that time. I believe they were kind of pissed that they still couldn't talk about Ebola because of me. Or the whole solar flare that never hit us like the scientist said. They were only a week off, by the way, from total blackout from all electricity and communication devices going dark for ten years or so. I think back at it now, what kind of world that would have become. The scientist said if it did hit us back then, we would still be feeling the effects of getting everything back online to this day.

They started getting angry and started calling me names in the media. They would talk about how this all started with a guy in a prison cell. But they did it in a way that the public wouldn't have known unless you knew about what was going on with my situation. Like calling me mommy's boy for instance. Or calling me evil. If this was real, I might as well play with them a little bit. I got in front of the TV and said with a smile on my face, "Sticks and stones will break my bones, but names will never hurt me," kind of in a childish way. Just to rev them up a little more.

A couple of hours went by, then I heard from the weather channel about this strange jet stream called Pineapple Express coming from Hawaii that was going to hit the Bay Area in California, which made me think about what I had said to my mom, that there's something about Bay Road, thinking that was the name of the road I grew up on. "Was it Bay Road?" Shaking my head in disbelief, I went to lunch.

When I got back to the rec room after lunch, I ran to the TV and turned on the news. I found out that the storm did hit the Bay Area. And there were massive landslides with boulders and tree limbs crushing houses out there. *That's so crazy*, I thought. But I could kind of see they were still trying to make fun of me, calling me evil.

When I turned my head to the TV really slowly and rubbed my hands over my face and said "sticks and stones" with a crooked grin on my face, I was getting immediate responses as I was going through channels in that rec room. When I turned to the next channel, they mentioned something about what I had said. "Did you hear him? He said sticks and stones?" Then after that, I felt the rage that was coming out from Hollywood was surreal.

They had a woman stand up looking really scared, singing "Silent Night," which, if you listen to the lyrics, was kind of creepy. It was as if she was singing it in such a way to threaten me. I never read too much into that song before, which I guess could have two different meanings. Does it mean the night outside is silent? Or a knight from the Dark Ages who is kept from talking and forbidden to speak? Sleeping in heavenly peace sounded like a threat to me. I was scared shitless, but if I told anyone about any of this, I think to this day I would still be locked away, wearing a straitjacket somewhere. After that, I didn't say anything else into that TV in the rec room and went to bed.

But I swear one crazy thing happened after another. There was something about all those planes that crashed that year or went missing. There was one that I remember in particular where a huge passenger plane in China took a nosedive out of the sky, not before its wing just slightly clipped a taxicab while the cab was driving down an expressway where the plane crashed into a basin. I don't think anyone died in the crash. It was some crazy footage. You should look it up sometime. I remember watching that footage in a dark room with twenty or so guys. It just looked fake for some reason, but it was so scary, as it was played over a news broadcast as everything else in this country was going on.

Or Harrison Ford's plane that he lost control of and crashed into some graveyard. They interviewed his son that day. He reassured everyone on the news by saying, "Don't worry, Dad is okay." How about that missing Malaysian 737 plane? There were a lot more planes that went down that year; those were just a few. Maybe it had to do with that solar flare that almost hit us. I guess it would have made something like that happen from what I heard. The solar flare could have messed with the location devices in these planes. The solar flare never did hit us that year like they said it would, so probably not.

Around this time, they were making the ruling on gay marriage, making gay marriage legal and binding and that it is a right for a gay couple to get married in a church. In a church! They couldn't just be happy enough to do it in a courthouse or something. They would get to stand in front of a priest, and they had to marry them even if it was against that priest's beliefs. It didn't seem fair to me. It did seem like the television already had this all planned with the gay commercials and gay videos coming out just days after the pope made that announcement. It would take a long time to film all those commercials. It did seem like someone gave them an inside word on what this ruling was going to be.

This is crazy, I thought. Why now, when there were already rioters all over America? With everything else going on at that time? Damn, it's like they were trying to get us to fight and kill each other. This must all be a plan. Obama made peace with Cuba too—I heard over the news—and he was talking on how a dictatorship in this country might not be that bad of a thing. That's it, I thought Obama and his cronies didn't want to leave. They wanted to stay in power to rule all who were left over after America's race war he was starting. Then he could even rewrite the constitution in such a way for the Democratic party to rule over us forever. Can you imagine back then if we were fighting COVID-19 instead of Ebola? I'm sure those elites pulling the strings would have gotten their way.

I think this whole thing with militarizing the police, taking away our guns, was all planned too. So maybe we wouldn't put up a fight. Even the way they were training the police, they were always talking about performance rather than service, which to me is what being a policeman was about. They were training these cops how to kill two taps to the chest to make sure that they're dead as if they were at war with us or something, rather than defusing the situation and calming everyone down without the use of deadly force. They were being trained to shoot first and ask questions later.

That's when I knew I could never come out with this whole rape-suicide story. Cause if I did, well, I don't know what would have happened. It would have given them a reason to fight back. I had an idea. I would have to say something so horrible that all these Christian speakers who were watching me and listening to me through that little camera so they would stay away from me.

I remember reading something in the Knights Templar book about the Indian mysticism. I remember thinking that I didn't know that was an actual thing. But I do remember how in their religion they used animals as one of their primary sources on how to relate to the human condition; what animal you act like is the spirt animal that you would come back as when you die.

I thought about it, and I had come up with something to say that would defuse this situation. So I thought about the Son of God riding an ass or a donkey down the mountain as it was foretold in prophesy. The guys were joking around, saying, "I want to be a real boy" for some reason I didn't know, which made me think of Pinocchio. I got out of my bed as Hagee truly wanted me to say something, listening to him over the radio. I went up to the TV and said, "Maybe those Indian mystics got it right. Maybe if you act like an ass, then maybe in the next life, you may turn into ass or a donkey, kind of like in Pinocchio." Then I waved my hand in front of my nose like my nose was getting longer. "You want a license to marry. How about a license to have a kid and when you have that kid, you to be sure to never leave that kid no matter what? Who am I to judge?" I said with some anger and rage in my voice. "Who are you to judge?" I said as I point at the TV. "You have these people in competition with each other on how many kids they're going to have with all this free money that you give them. All this fighting in all these different countries. All these countless wars, for what? Because we think our religion is so great. Most people who join the military didn't want to kill anyone. All they wanted was money for college."

Then I stood up and went back in my room. I put the earbuds on and started to cry a little bit 'cause I knew what I had just said was right but very wrong at the same time. I knew that there would be no chance for me to be protected by the church, and I was on my own. I didn't hear too much out of Hagee after that, but there was another preacher talking to me in there. His name was James MacDonald. I remember him saying, "Don't worry, son of God, your stone's throw will never be forgotten" and that I was one of his people. That I changed something down here that could not be measured.

Then I switched over to a local station, and this disc jockey was talking about that. He just let out a rebel yell, then started talking to a lady and telling her not to act like a jackass, and they both started to laugh. *Damn, these guys are talking about me too*, I thought. It took every ounce of me not to freak out. What if all this was a hallucination from the lack of sleep I was having here? What if what I was witnessing was all just a coincidence. Nobody was talking to me. The guards were all just giving me dirty looks at the time. With no way to know for sure, I still didn't know what I was going through in here was real or not.

CHAPTER 8

Confirmation

That night, though, one of the guards on the way to chow looked at me and nodded, then started to shake around. "Better watch out for that Ebola."

"What's that matter, Sarge? You got that Ebola in you?"

"Sure do seems like that way to me," one of the guards said, then they shared a laugh. The guard that was leading us the cafeteria started to whistle the Guns N' Roses song "Patience." He seemed to be whistling it for me at the time as he lined us up for chow that night.

The other guards seemed to be not uptight as well and started to give me nods instead of dirty looks that I was used to. But nobody came out to say anything. They all would just smile and give me nods. Well, at least I felt more at ease with these guards instead of encountering me with all this hate and rage all the time.

There was something on the TV when I came back from chow that reminded me of an old saying, so I spoke into the TV. It was another message to those elites who was watching me. "There is no *I* in team." Crazy, as soon as I said that, though, I was watching a cage match between two fighters in an MMA match where one of the competitors was nicknamed Nostradamus. I swear he looked into the camera and put one finger on his lips like he was giving me a sign to be quiet. Like the cosmic force or AI system really didn't want me to say that there is no *I* in the team.

That's when I got the slip to see the psychiatrist. They always knew exactly the right time to send me there. "Okay," I said to myself. "Don't say anything stupid, Sam. You're almost out of here." I knew if I were to open my mouth about any of this, she would lock me away for sure. So I sat down with her.

"How's everything going, Sam?" she said as she smiled, and she almost seemed to be gloating.

"I'm good."

"Anything you want to talk about.?"

"No, I'm just here to answer any of your questions."

"Okay then, so that's it."

"Well then," I shook my head, talking to myself. "I don't want to talk about that." Then I looked at her and said, "What I saw when I came here was some kind of a race war instead of everyone coming together in peace."

"Everything worked out better than you expected, didn't it, Cole?" she said.

I started to stand up and said, "Yes, it did." Then I went on to say, "I feel really sorry for those counselors over there at the treatment center. They must have had a hard time growing up as a kid, especially in junior high" as I smiled while I walked out her door.

I knew that was kind of mean, but I felt that it needed to be said considering what they were doing to those guys in there still.

Personally, I didn't know how the TV was doing it. It was like it was throwing a temper tantrum over the fact that I played a trick down there to protect the protesters. I really wanted that $5 million, but if I were to say what I was thinking in there, they would label me crazy for sure. They would get the press and expose me and the story of Officer Holt.

I started going to the yard a lot more after that and exercising around anything to get me away from this TV. Playing basketball with the guys was fun since I'm tall. I was okay; I held my own. From the back it was always hard to tell who was on my team, though. I kept passing to the wrong guy with everyone having the same haircut and all. But it was fun. There were basketball tournaments. Soccer tournaments, handball courts. I did a lot of running on the track.

I would run a mile a day. I had this sit-up technique too that I was doing in here. I learned in grade school "left elbow right knee, right elbow left knee." It seemed to balance my brain out a little bit and help with this empty void feeling I was having all the time.

Still, all these little white rabbits in there were tripping me out. They would come right up to you and not be afraid at all. But all in all, the place seemed to be more of a retirement community than a prison. There were some guys who, when they got let go, didn't want to leave. They were throwing fits, yelling and screaming, sometimes even crying. I just looked at them in disbelief. They did have all their friends in here, though, and they didn't have to work. So I guess I didn't blame them considering how bad Chicago was right now.

There were some strange weather anomalies out there with different-looking clouds forming on the horizon all the time with more sky than ground to look at. I guess I just wasn't used to seeing all this sky. All of it seemed more fake than real. Like whatever I had done put me in a different dimension of time or something. The prison started to have a blackbird problem too. I swear the birds would take over half of the soccer field when we got out to the yard. All you saw was black on the field. It was funny watching them, though. The last row of birds would fly in front of the first row and would move down the whole field that way, which kind of looked like a huge game of leapfrog.

After witnessing these crazy anomalies, at the end of my rec time, I always had to go back to my bunk. Damn, the timing every time I looked at the TV. When are they going to stop playing that *Mockingjay* preview? "I have a message for you, President Snow. If we're going to burn...then you're going to burn with us." That preview seemed to be coming out of the TV every time Jennifer Lawrence said it. Then I thought, *Mockingjay. Why did they have to call that movie that? Am I mocking J, meaning Jesus, for what I'm doing in here? Is this all relative?*

Stop it, Sam. I had a deck of cards. Playing solitaire at the time was helping me out, trying not to look at the TV. Something had come to my head that made a lot of sense to me. I said, "The only control that I have are these cards that I have in front of me. And the only rule that is most important is not to cheat, which, if you think about it, is a good philosophy in life as well."

MTV had a new music video come on TV about playing solitaire. Right away I thought, *What the hell.* Maybe I was starting to look much into all of this like looking into the sky and seeing faces in the clouds or something. There was something about all of it that just seemed so supernatural and frightening. Something really did not want me to leave that place; something was trying to keep me there, and it was trying to push me off my rocker. Believe me, they were doing a good job. All I could do was watch as if it was fake, as if I were in the middle of a horror movie; but one thing for certain was that I couldn't flinch.

That cosmic force was pissed that I tricked it. And what made it worse was that I wasn't that smart of a guy, never attending college and all. I bet it was like losing a game of chess to a little kid or something. I felt that rage when I lost sometimes too, and it didn't feel good. But I had no idea how I could become such a good player. It was like the cosmic pushes were leading me here all my life. He or it was testing me with this hand that I was dealt. My ability not to cheat was me telling the truth. The truth shall set you free, and I was hoping it was going to work like the Bible said so I could make it back to my daughter.

Then I turned to one of the guys, and I said maybe this was all a bet. A bet between me and God. Maybe it was all just a little wager that there was no way that I was going to make it through. Was this all a maze? I knew now all I had to do was hold on for two more months, and I could live out my days at home with my baby girl.

Every day spent there was torture. For months on end, there was no porn, no way to relieve myself. With twenty or so guys per room, there was no way to do it in your bed. So they would take turns going to the bathroom with a magazine one of them snuck in. I'm telling you; I know this sounds gross, but it has to be said. When I was here, I had a tent pitched in my pants every night when I went to bed and every morning when I woke up. It makes sleeping here nearly impossible. You would do anything to make it go away.

I did a lot of my sit-ups and jumping jacks just to keep my mind off sex. I was in some deep-seated warrior mode. Some definite spiritual warfare was going on in here, and there was nothing that would keep me from going home to see my kid. I wasn't going to let them win. I felt I had to be in tip-top shape to take on whatever I was fighting in here. So I didn't touch myself inappropriately once in the six months that I was here. It was the hardest thing I had ever done, no pun intended.

There would be some weird dreams that I was having almost on a nightly basis. There would be this hot chick taking my clothes off and doing some sexual things to me. Then after I pushed her away saying I have a wife at home, she would turn into this black-haired, green-eyed witch. The dream still haunts me to this day. I can still see her face change, and I still remember what that lady looked like in that dream all those years ago.

One morning I had a conversation with my bunkmate in front of the TV.

"I don't know who I'm fighting in here," I said to him. "I don't even think it's the warden. Theres some kind evil force in here. I don't know what it is." Then I started shadowboxing the air like I was fighting someone in the room that was invisible. Shadowboxing around the room, I probably looked like I lost my damn mind. "Do you hear me? You're not going to get me. Not without a fight. Who are you? Show yourself." I made sure I was talking in front of that TV, hoping someone was spying on me early this morning. I had this feeling that I was communicating with someone else other than my cellie or the people behind that camera.

It's crazy, though, that an hour or two later that morning, at chow time, I sat across the lunch table from an inmate whom I had never seen before with devil horn tattoos on his forehead. No joke. When I looked at his name tag, it read Russell Witherbee, which to me at the time sounded a lot like "wrestling with me," as if I were wrestling with the devil.

I asked him what made him get those horns on his head. He gave me a half-crooked smile and said it seemed like a good idea at the time. He said he was part of a gang, which in so many ways made him feel more validated. I told him when he got out of here and he went on a job interview, to be sure to wear a hat. He smiled a little bit and said that if he planned on ever getting a job, he would never have gotten them in the first place. "Right," I said. He seemed like a nice enough guy when I talked with him, but he looked to me like something out of a Rob Zombie movie.

He turned to me and said, "Hey, look, it's the warden, and he's out of his cage." Only seeing the warden a couple of times since I had been here, it did seem kind of weird seeing him in the cafeteria. We never made eye contact, but he seemed kind of jumpy. Then I saw him talking to one of the other inmates in the chow line, and he started shadowboxing around as if he were fighting the air. The same thing I was doing. Maybe he was watching me a little while ago shadowboxing, but he looked as if he was scared jumping around with wide eyes. I still had no proof that he was watching me or listening to me, so I couldn't tell for sure if he was reacting to me or not.

After lunch, when I got back, I started talking with the other guys in there as if there was a recording device in here, asking guys what they were in here for. There was a guy serving twenty years dealing crack. Then I said to him, "It doesn't matter if you smoke cocaine or snort cocaine. It still turns you into a fiend. It's just one gets you there faster than the other one. Look at what these doctors are doing, handing out prescriptions with any little pain you have. I once got a big bottle of OxyContin for a toothache.

"Look at all these doctors and pharmaceutical companies that are getting rich off all these drugs that are killing people, and they're getting away with it. Then there are drugs like coke and crack, very rarely kills anyone, and guys like you who are selling those type of drugs lose half of their life in here over a couple of eight balls. It just doesn't make sense to me. Well, I guess these pharmaceutical companies have enough money to buy politicians who put these laws into place."

"Damn, Cole, you're right," one of the guys said. "But nothing is going to change as long as they're making all this money off of us being in here and billions off everyone else out there. Why would they want that to change?"

I said, "You know, they should just make all drugs legal. Just stay away from the pharmaceutical ones because those are the ones that will kill you."

With all the TVs in there, it was hard not to look at all of them. They had police brutality protests all over the United States for the whole time I was here. It seemed like hundreds of thousands of Americans took to the streets over the grand jury decisions regarding the death of Michael Brown, and New York regarding the death of Eric Garner who was saying he could not breathe as a cop choked him and killed him. I remember Eric Garner being extremely over-weight, which most likely had something to do with his death, but maybe I'm wrong. I remember telling someone it looked like the sky was falling out there.

There were so many bad decisions cops were making at the time. It was the training, I thought. I remember they switched the way they trained new recruits after all of this, even old-school cop TV shows at the time. Do you remember how violent they used to be? It's a lot different nowadays on *Live PD*.

It seemed to be all caught on camera, and they were being shown all at the same time as if the media was gaslighting all the protesters as if it were some sort of master plan. I was blaming it on the militarized training of the police at the time. When video cameras seemed to be in everyone's hands, a new video camera on an iPhone, which the police couldn't get away with anymore, because it was right there on camera.

But still, there were so many around that time. There was a twelve-year-old Tamir Rice shot dead by police in November. Then there was Akai Gurley. There were so many stories that came out in a short amount of time that it just seemed endless. They were saying that the protests were mostly peaceful. But the images in the footage I was watching footage were similar to those of the movie *Soylent Green*. The protesters seemed to be looting all the stores, setting fire to all their commodities.

But in between all the rioting, the politicians would try to calm the protesters down by saying the training of the police officers have got to get back from the Perforomist-based training to protect-and-serve-based training that was meant to be. Then I heard they were going to make it mandatory for all officers to wear body cameras.

Maybe they were watching me from the beginning because that is exactly what I had been saying—word for word—since I got here. Or maybe it was the letter. I almost forgot about the letter that I had given to the work camp warden. He must have given it to those women at the Ferguson town hall meetings. This lady was talking about the fear-based society that we're living in and that we all must calm down and stop being so scared of one another. She even said and used the black and blue profiling term that I came up with. Personally, I didn't care if I got no credit as long as the loss of life was as low as it was. I was happy.

Between all the riots, Ebola, solar flares, space quakes, all those planes falling and disappearing out of sky, all these weather anomalies, there were all these movie stars' deaths too. There was a lot to fear that year, and what with looking at twenty or so hellish scenes of craziness on the TVs, it just seemed like it was a lot more reason to believe that hell on earth had arrived.

But as I was thinking about this, I could only imagine how worst off the situation would have been if I was talking on that screen about this place or Officer Holt and that poor rape victim. What if that became front and center in the news media at that time. I kept my mouth shut and stayed off the phone. I believed at the time that was the only thing that was keeping the cops and the militant officers from using brutal force on everyone.

All of this can't be true, I thought to myself. *Maybe I'm in a controlled social experiment, and everyone in here is in on it except for me.* Or maybe I was dreaming or hallucinating from the lack of sleep because I heard that could happen. It just seemed too crazy to be true even looking back on this now.

After New Year's, I felt like there was some sort of destination made. Or I felt as if we made it. It was 2015, a new year, a new day, and I felt good about it. I do remember watching TV toward the end of my stay. I watched someone talking about race and that we're all basically the same people with different life experiences, that's all. Some just had more pigment in their skin than others. And to judge a person by the contents of their character, not by the color of their skin, is the only way to go through life. I do remember looking right into the TV, saying, "Thank you, guys."

After that was a roll call for breakfast. *Good*, I thought. I was starving. I got my breakfast for the day and sit down at one of the twenty or so tables in the cafeteria. Then out of nowhere came these two guys dressed in suits and long trench coats. I right away thought these guys were the Feds. That's what they looked to me. It was as if they came out of a movie set or something out of nowhere. They were talking to the warden. The warden looked as if he was in trouble, waving his hands about like a little kid who was trying to get out of trouble. After they stopped talking to him, the two guys in suits and long trench coats shared a grin and started to walk toward me. We made eye contact, but I quickly looked away. I kind of felt intimidated. They proceeded to just walk right past me, smiling as I was sitting down eating my eggs and toast. Then they walked around my lunch table without saying anything to me and proceeded to walk back to the warden.

I knew what that meant. They were watching me just a few minutes ago when I said, "Thank you, guys." And it was their way to say thank you back and that they were watching me and not to be afraid when I left, that I would be okay and no one was going to kill me. How I got that from a nod and a smile, I couldn't tell you. But I felt that they didn't have to say anything; that was enough for me to feel validated and less afraid. How many people and who were watching me in that rec room through that camera in there, I'll never know. It did seem as if they were showing their appreciation for what I did.

"Isn't that weird?" the inmate next to me said. "Why would those two FBI guys walk around only our table and not say anything. There's something going on around here." All I could do was nod because of the fear I had inside of me starting to grow, what with this being more of a confirmation. What I was experiencing all this time was, in fact, real, and it wasn't just my mind playing tricks on me from the lack of sleep I was getting.

After the FBI walked around the table, the warden led them out, still moving around as if he were in trouble. As the warden was holding the doors open for those FBI guys, just before the warden left through those doors, he looked back at me with one glance before he left. It was all it took for me. It was almost as if I could read his face. It read, "How in the hell this dumb white kid from the suburbs ever get the better of me?"

I almost felt sorry for him, but I knew in my heart that his intentions of running this prison were not good. Messing with a person's release date and having them perform tasks as the prison sees fit are unacceptable. If you think about it, you will do anything to get back to your family if all it would take is to become a Chistian like them, or to humiliate yourself to a group of guys by standing in front of them and do a little dance, or to study from books that they see fit. It was a trap, and the only way that I knew how to play was to not play at all and accept my full sentence and do my time with my head held high.

I believe that had been their plan all along, to get people angry enough so there would be an endless flow of inmates to take care of maybe so then they would have some sort of job security here. With the prison system being their number one source of income in this town, they were greedy; and hell, I wouldn't be surprised if the stockholders in the prison system had something to do with all this too. It wouldn't surprise me 'cause to them it's all about making as much money as they can. Damn whoever stands in their way. Letting violent offenders go early on what they call good time and letting simple traffic offenders sit and wait to their final day of their sentence. Yet this is just one inmate's opinion of this whole prison system, just another way for these private prison institutions to make money. The worse off society gets out there, the more money they make in prison.

When I left the cafeteria, gunshots rang out. I knew that they were doing this on purpose. Every time I stepped out either to go to the yard or the cafeteria, there would be gunshots. Those watchtower guys, I swear, would order gunshots to be fired at the gun range next door exactly the time when I got out of that cafeteria. I swear they loved to see me jump and duck for cover. They got me every time. I could see them laughing at me in their tower. It could be my nerves and what with everything going on. Then I would see these signs in the yard that read, "You'd better to follow orders, or you will be shot," so can you blame me? I bet they would have loved to be able to just end my life right there and call it an accident. Maybe just say that I was trying to escape or something. Maybe then they could escape any kind of national embarrassment about what was going on here.

When I got back to my bunk, I looked at the date, and it was reaching the end of January. *Just three more weeks*, I thought. Come on, Sam, you can do it. Just then, as I was thinking that, the preview of *Unbroken* came on: "Go get them, you stupid dago." This place was driving me to the brink.

I would listen to songs on the radio too. Then I would make comparisons of what I was going through here. This one radio station played a lot of Beatles music. As I was listening to one of their songs, I couldn't help but think of my situation. It was a song by Paul McCartney "Band on the Run."

> Well, the undertaker drew a heavy sigh
> Seeing no one else had come
> And a bell was ringing in the village square
> For the rabbits on the run
> Band on the run
> Band on the run
> And the jailer man and Sailor Sam
> Were searching everyone for the band on the run
> And the county judge who held a grudge

It was all just a little too creepy. They were even singing about rabbits being on the run. And sailor Sam—was it me who was sailing through time for me to get to this spot at this time? Man, I needed to get out of here. I was thinking about the creative cosmic force that had been pushing me my whole life for this fight that I was fighting right here and now.

Then there would be these old movies that would be playing in the rec room too like the movie *12 Monkeys*. It's about a time traveler from the future, played by Bruce Willis, who tries to stop a global pathogen from killing everyone on the planet. Now why does his name have to be Cole? It is a good movie. As I was watching, I was thinking about the craziness that reminded me a lot of what was going on. I didn't have a radio in here until the end of my stay, and listening to these old songs made me feel like Bruce Willis did when he was singing that song: "I found my thrill on Blueberry Hill, on Blueberry Hill when I found you." Then he started to cry his eyes out. And I couldn't help from doing the same, thinking how much God or my subconscious had been speaking with me. I quickly got back to my bunk before any of the other guys saw my face.

"What's wrong, Cole?" my cellie asks.

"Nothing, bud. Just missing my family," I said.

"Yeah, me too," he said. Without trying to say anything else, I let the conversation go silent as I wiped these crazy tears from my eyes. That is what I felt in here. It was so evil yet so beautiful at the same time. It was so painful, yet I felt so at ease because I knew what I had done worked out in my favor and the protesters' as well. It was one crazy ride that no hallucinogenic drug could compare with.

Now before I knew what numerology was, I would be reading any set of random numbers like room numbers and combined with the bed numbers, and I would look them up in the Bible, and I would read that passage as if angles were talking to me and giving me direction on how to handle this story and situation that I was in. It kept pushing me and telling me I was meant to even the score down here.

I truly felt I found what I was looking for in here by keeping Jesus strictly in my heart, Pythagoras in my mind, and Buddha in my gut. God just seemed to make a lot more sense to me, which led me to my inner voice that had a lot of things to say to me so I could change this one event. Yet I couldn't forget about Indian mysticism, because without worshipping Mother Earth, we wouldn't have any kind of life to speak of without her. We must protect her.

I got called in one last time to the psychologist as what my slip read, which was lying on my bed. It read, "2:00 to 2:30." I really didn't want to go. I left without knowing how late I was until I entered the room. She asked me if there was anything more I wanted to add. I said no, I found what I was looking for and sorry that I lost track of time. Right at that moment, the second hand hit 12. It was 2:30, the exact time I was meant to leave. With her hand shaking vigorously, she wrote down every word I had said. Then she said with a crackle in her voice, "Take care, Mr. Cole." That's when I gave her a nod, then left.

As I was walking back to my bunk, I began to think. Maybe when I said that I lost track of time, she got a little freaked out. I don't know. Track of time, come to think of it, could hold some kind of alternative meaning, I guess. The timing of everything that I was going through on that track of time was so perfectly timed. It would have been a lot different for everyone if I were on a different track of time. Then I began to think about when I was in that treatment center and the things I said about being on a cosmic push, which made a lot more sense now than it did back then when this whole thing started.

CHAPTER 9

Homeward Bound

I was made to sit down to watch a reinduction film on what you should be doing when an inmate gets released. I was made to sit down with everyone else who was getting released that day. I sat down. It seemed like a newer film, like it had just been made. The guy in the video kind of made me laugh. He mentioned that he had no problem being on film and that he didn't know why anyone would if they got the chance, as if he were taking a shot at me. He also mentioned that when you leave, make sure that you wear protection when you have sex and that when you leave here, you still have a long road ahead with parole. Then he talked about having no guns and no dogs 'cause they could come over unannounced at any time and raid your house when you were on parole. I had never heard of anything like that, but I nodded to the teacher who was showing the film. When I left, I looked at her as if to say that I would comply. But instead of looking at me and smiling, she quickly turned her head away as if to say she was too scared of me to look at me.

At this point, I was expecting to get killed when I left, but I couldn't let anyone know that, what with the fear of people just thinking I was nuts. After handing in all my state clothes they gave me, they gave me street clothes to put on.

After I was done getting dressed, the two ministers from Jehovah's Witnesses just so happened to be entering the exact time I was leaving. I truly didn't think it was all by chance. I was only brave enough to give them a quick glance as they stared at me. I felt like I should have told them something, like "How did I do, guys?" but nothing came out. I knew I couldn't say anything. I needed to take a leap of faith. There would have been nothing that these ministers would be able to do to protect me anyway. I just bit my tongue and tried to ignore them as they stared at me.

There were two other inmates I was leaving with when I left. This one guy took one look at me and asked me what's wrong. I told him I was a little shaky from the lack of sleep I was getting in there. But I think he could tell that there was something else that was wrong. I probably looked like a guy who was about to be sent to the gallows, which in my mind was exactly what was going on. Before we left, there was a lady there who took my picture before. When she got done taking my digital picture, she looked down and compared the three pictures she had taken of me over the months. She took some time looking at them, then had a concerned face, which then almost turned white. Then she looked up at me and quietly said, "Don't you ever come back here."

I didn't hear her, so I said, "What's that?"

"Don't you ever come back here, Cole," she yelled at me as she pushed me out the door. *Well, that was kind of disturbing*, I thought. What was that about? What did she see in those pictures she took of me? Maybe it was for the best that I didn't know.

We got on the bus after that, and the driver of the bus took us to the train station. And all the way, I kept thinking, *So when is it going to happen? Are they going to wait till I'm alone, or are they going to make it look like an accident? Who knows? Just be brave, Sam. If they are going to take you out, don't let them see that you have any fear.*

After I got off the train from Springfield, I still had to take another train from Chicago to Round Lake. With a big box in hand with all my personal belongings inside and a prison hoodie on, there was no question where I had just come from.

Looking kind of out of control and scared walking in circles, I was thinking there had to be someone watching me because what seemed to me like an FBI agent started to walk up and talk to me. He said, "Calm down. Are you okay?" I nodded. "Let me see your ticket," he said. I told him I was going to buy the ticket on the train. "Well, he said, "looks like you just missed the five-o'clock train." He said that I would have to wait there for an hour to catch the next one. I thanked him, and he went on his way.

Maybe I wasn't going to get taken out or killed. My conversation with him seemed to have calmed me down, so I sat down and rested and waited for my train. I must have fallen asleep because when I opened my eyes, the clock read five minutes to six. I got up and ran to my train, got in, and sat down. The train conductor came over to me and said, "Seven dollars, please." I only had $5. Luckily, he was cool. He looked me over and noticed where I had come from. He gave me a nod and punched my ticket for me. After thanking him, I sat down and let out a long breath.

Well, only three hours away, I thought, *and I get to see Olivia and my Tammy. I missed them. I haven't spoken to them over the phone in months.* I really didn't want to let them know anything about the hard time that I had in there. Five years of silence? That's going to be tough. There was no way. There had to be more to it than this.

I finally got back to the house after walking five miles from the train station. The first thing I said to Tammy was, "I'm I too late."

"I don't know," she said. "I haven't heard from you in months. They told me you were getting out today."

"I know, I'm sorry. I didn't want to talk to anyone in there with the embarrassment of where I was at," I said. "Where is she at?"

"She's in the bath. She's excited to see you," Tammy said.

"So, does Olivia know where I was?"

"I told her that you were working out of state. I told her that was good." It seemed like forever till she got out of the bath. But when she did, it was as if she didn't recognize me. She became really shy and started running around. I followed her to our bedroom, and she grabbed a book.

"Da Da, can you read to me?" she said as she looked at me with her wide blue eyes. I started to tear up hearing her speak to me for the first time face-to-face. I did read her that book, and it reminded me of all the times since she was born when I read it to her. But this time was the first time, I believe, that she could understand the words I was speaking as well as the tone of my voice.

Well, the cable news and TV changed when I got out. Instead of three world news organizations that were only talking about what was happening around the world, there were like eight including Al Jazeera, and it was all about politics and actual world news and what was happening around the world, which seemed so foreign to me. They even had C-SPAN where I could see my congressman live. Before that day, I didn't even know who or what they looked like.

The commercials weren't talking about DUIs as much either but had a couple commercials about distracted driving and that is how you shouldn't be on social media when you're trying to drive your kid around. They stopped showing old reruns of *Cops*, too, where a lot of the time they had white cops arresting and tackling inner-city black youth as they always seemed to be trying to get away from them. They had *Live PD* where mostly black cops were going after black suspects.

The C-SPAN channel was going full force attack mode on opioids too. They were finally starting to take a hard look at these companies and doctors who sold them to people who were getting addicted to these drugs. See, Congress had been looking in the other direction for so long with all the kickbacks that they were getting from these companies. It looked like they finally had enough, and some major legislation was coming down to stop them from doing this to us.

I left, but it seemed to just get worse out there as soon as I turned on the news. There were about three or four big oil tanker train explosions that week. I don't know. They all seemed to be carrying oil. It looked so apocalyptic out there. It was in all different parts of the country. There must have been three or four within two or three days. It could have been a coincidence, but it didn't seem like it, though, like it was a sign that we should stop it with all the fossil fuels that we were using.

President Obama came on the screen. He was walking over the Selma bridge in Alabama, commemorating the bloody Sunday attack on black protesters by the police, which happened fifty years ago to the day. It seemed like a big coincidence considering all the race riots that were going on in the country at the time. It was a completely different scene this time, though. Black people got to protest peacefully without the cops brutally attacking them. I couldn't help to think if I hadn't done what I had done, it might have been a different scene down there, maybe even a repeat of the massacre that happened back then. I don't know. It's crazy to think like that.

Then after walking over that bridge, President Obama gave a speech after serving eight years in office. He never mentioned how far we had come as a country, being the first black president and all. He was only talking more about racism and how this march wasn't over, that there was a lot more we needed to accomplish. I don't know with this guy. I would have thought that after becoming the first black president in the White House, white Americans would finally stop from being called racist in this country all the time. He was in the White House for eight years. It seemed to me that with all the looting and violent protests that were going on at the time, he could have done a better job calming people down and bringing the races together. It just seemed like he was gaslighting the situation and separating us more with his words. To me that's what a lot of democrats do. They use our compassion for other people against us as a weapon so they can stay in power. It seems like everyone in this country is a victim with the exception of white males.

If you're white and male, forget about it. With this affirmative action or diversity training, good luck becoming a UPS driver. It takes six years to become one. In contrast, a black or Hispanic takes only two years to do so, according to my brother when he was trying to get in over there. There are countless other examples. It's all over. The only racism I see is against white noncollege educated males trying to compete in an unbalanced workforce. It's hard when you're trying to make something out of yourself and gets shot down because of your skin color. Now in my eyes that's the true definition of the word *racist*. What did Martin Luther King say? Judge not by color of your skin but by the content of their character. When you're not competing against one another not by a merit-based system but instead giving people a leg up for the color of their skin, you can't call it by any other name but racism.

My brother has a clean driving record and is one of the nicest guys I know. But he was told that it didn't matter because he was the wrong color even though he was competing against these guys who had blemishes all over their driving records.

I just believe in freedom of hiring whoever you think would be best qualified to fill that position, not to be forced to hire a less qualified person just because of their race. Sorry, guys, I don't believe that I'm racist. The policies we all must follow are. Okay, where was I at?

Oh yeah, I was happy about finally being back home spending time with my daughter. It was nearly a year and a half since I saw her last. She could almost talk in full sentences now. Tammy was still working full-time, and with me not being able to drive and a parole officer coming to the house all the time, I was going to be the stay-at-home dad for the two years I was on parole.

It was nice. My daughter and I would ride bikes to the park. She had this carriage thing that would attach to the back of my bike, and we would just play all day long. I would make voices for her stuffed animals and make up songs for her. She really liked that. I always had dinner ready for everyone. I also did the laundry and dishes. I could do this, I thought. It seemed pretty easy. I didn't have cravings for cigarettes or alcohol either. I wasn't stressed out from work, and my body didn't hurt from working all day. There was no need to drink or do drugs.

My parole officer didn't like that too much, though. "You can't just be a stay-at-home dad," he would say. "What are you going to do about money? And there is this treatment program court mandate hanging over your head."

"Without a driver's license and a job to pay for it, treatment will be hard to do," I said.

He said that he would talk to the judge and his superiors about removing the mandate. When he got back to me days later, his superiors agreed that I would be exempted, meaning that I wouldn't have to do treatment. Thank God, I thought. With everything I had gone through in there, I felt like I had been through enough.

Basically, all I had to do was call in once a week to check in and be home when my parole officer told me to. Being home sometimes was terrible for me. From being used to working fifty to sixty hours a week to waking up at four in the morning. I still got up at four, but now I was twiddling my thumbs, waiting for Olivia to wake up, which could be as late as ten. It was a big change for me and left me a lot of time to myself. So naturally, I would turn on the TV.

Watching normal, sane people lose their minds was always entertaining for me. Mainstream media broadcasters didn't seem to be in control of the narrative anymore and lied to us. Because now there were way more than three other news organizations on TV. There was like twenty, all of them trying to catch each other lying. Their fact-checkers were always trying to disprove the competitions' fact-checkers. With Obama as president, the only thing the news would be talking about was how great the man was without ever taking a good look at his policies and how much they hurt the American people. Or how he pushed race down our throats for eight years as soon as something didn't go his way.

I was having a good laugh, but at the same time I was scared to death. Movie stars were angry because nobody cared about them as much anymore. Politicians were angry 'cause now they would become the center of attention and the media would find out every little detail of their lives. Theologians and Christian speakers were angry too.

Well, at least Hagee was. He seemed to be taking shots at me all over the place, telling his parishioners that if they don't know what they're talking about, then they should shut up and that people weren't supposed to take the best out all the world's religions and make something of their own. Crazy, I thought, I almost had him join forces with me. Then he went on to say that he knows who the Antichrist is, that he is so well hidden and that he is not what we think he is. The rage behind his eyes was scary as he talked, like he was talking to me through the TV. I could only watch him for so long that I would have to switch the channel.

I would watch Catholic priests, though. They would come out talking about how maybe the only place for Jesus to be is the heart.

And they would reference something in the Bible and why they were saying so. One priest went on to say that there is a lot we all can learn from other religions and that we should always keep our minds open and always listen to what your conscience is telling you.

Then this other one came on and said that maybe we are all jackasses holding up the Lord and maybe that is not necessarily a bad thing, which made me feel bad for what I had said back in Jacksonville. I just wanted them to get off my back down there, not for other people to feel bad about their religion. There are a lot of good things about worshipping Jesus. But it also has a lot of weird practices that are on the verge of being just crazy. I did feel sorry for the man preaching on TV, but I also felt that what I said back in Jacksonville needed to be said.

I would turn the channel, and there would be this whole episode about the American Indians and what they had to say about population growth that the Catholic religion supported all these years. This Indian would come on the screen with tears while they showed footage of modern inner-city life.

Then they had white people trying to figure out all their practices with the drums and teaching them how they meditated, teaching them about their headdress, and all their beliefs. They went on and on, saying we should be looking more toward the Indians if we were to have any kind of future on this planet.

I was watching Bill Meyer, and I would be listening to what he had to say about what was going on. He was making jokes about how it seemed like everyone forgot how to fly airplanes with all the planes falling out of the sky recently. Then he started to talk about religion and how not to mess with other people's religion. When you prove someone that they're wrong with their beliefs, they will never forgive you for that. Then he was showing clips of Sara Palin ranting and raving, which did seem like she was talking about me. "Does he think that now it's okay? That it's teatime now?" It's the Boston Tea Party time, which meant that I wasn't going to talk, and she was mad that I was comfortably back home now drinking my tea. Then Bill Meyer said, "Doesn't she remind you of a girl who doesn't want to leave the party late at night high on cocaine?" I found that pretty funny.

With every passing day, there would be something on TV that would remind me about what I said in prison. So I was getting a little paranoid around this time, looking out the window and wondering if this day was going to be the day that I would have the media all over my front lawn.

All of this couldn't be true. It had to be some sort of strange coincidence, I thought. But time and time again, every time there would be some newscaster talking about a revolution, and it started with this kid in a prison cell, then they would be quickly interrupted and saying that they weren't supposed to talk about that. And that guy didn't exist. I just felt crazier and crazier.

What was the craziest about all of this is when that cop Joe Gliniewicz from Fox Lake was found dead off on Sayton Road near the police station in the woods soon after I was released. I lived across the street from that police station in a place called Devlin apartments. It was on Devlin Road, which almost connected to the Sayton Road, the road where he was found dead. For a few years, when I was in my twenties, I lived across the street from that police station with my live-in girlfriend. The TV went berserk over that one.

It went along with what I was talking about to my mom back in Jacksonville, like I was being pushed on a cosmic level. It was taking me back and coming out in a way and was using the streets that I lived on to communicate with me. With a road called Devlin, it almost had devil in its name. Then he died on Sayton Road as if the devil himself was giving people a message to come look for me. The news organization was going nuts over this one. I could tell.

That police officer Joe was found dead in the woods a few blocks from the police station. Then right before he died, he went over dispatch that he was following three suspects. Then he led the dispatcher to believe that he was under attack. The police department had other police come in from different departments, looking for the murderer. They had SWAT teams on top of schools. It was a real mess. Then they came on TV saying that there would be an award for anyone who had information about what had happened.

It made international news. I had to change the channel because of how insane it was getting out there.

Just as I started to change to a different channel, when I looked outside my house, I saw about ten cars pulling up to my house. I thought, *Okay, here we go.* When I looked outside, it was dark, and I couldn't tell what kind of cars they were, but I didn't see flashing lights, so I knew that was a good sign.

About eight guys came to my door. Tammy was there with my baby girl. One guy seemed to be in charge. When I opened the door, he asked if I was Sam. I said I was. Then Athena, my dog, came up barking at him snarling. "Get back, Athena," I yelled. One of the guys behind the guy who knocked on the door pulled out a gun. I forgot that one of my conditions said no vicious dogs to be allowed at my home while I was serving my time on parole. He started to giggle.

"It's only a Pomeranian," he said to the officer who had his gun out. "There's more hair than dog. Put that gun away."

"Damn, guys, I have a little kid here," I said. That's when I told Tammy to take Olivia and go to the living room, that I would handle this.

When I opened the door, they pushed themselves inside. Then the guy who seemed to be in charge asked me, "You don't mind if we come in, do you?"

"I guess not," I said. Then about ten people followed behind him. There seemed to be only two officers with about eight other plain-clothed people with guns who rushed in. They didn't say where they were from. But he did say that they weren't part of any local police department or part of the prison parole board. About eight guys and two women came barging through my house and started to search through my house. Now what they were searching for, I didn't know. I wish I would have asked what organization they were a part of, but they kept me busy answering their questions.

"She's tall. How old is she?" one of the women asked as she got done searching the house.

"My daughter is two, ma'am," I said as Olivia's little feet pounded on the wooden floor when she ran off to her brother's room. "Tammy, get Olivia. Keep her in the living room," I yelled.

Then the guy in charge started to become more demanding with his questions. "Have a seat, sir." With me standing almost a foot over him, I didn't blame him for wanting me to sit down. It was hard for me to take orders from someone who just barged into my house, but I sat down at my kitchen table as he started to grill me.

"What do you do for a living?" he asked.

"A painter," I said.

"A painter, yeah right. If you're a painter, what kind of brush do you use?"

"A Purdy brush, sir."

He looked over his shoulder at his partner, and he said, "That is my favorite brush too."

"Purdy's are the best," his partner said. The other guy in the room said that he wished that he were a painter as he started telling me about his side jobs and his projects at his house. They could tell I was starting to get frustrated. So they began to start asking me the questions that they came here to ask.

"So, haven't you been watching the TV?" the guy in charge asked. I said yes. It's hard to explain what seemed like small talk. I believe they were trying to size me up and wanted me to come out and say what was on their minds. But I wasn't going to. I tried the best I could to make them believe everything they were witnessing on the TV was just a coincidence, and I was a nobody.

He went on to ask about Joe Gliniewicz and if I had something to do with his death. I told him I had nothing to do with it. But he stared me down as if I was lying to him or that I had something I was hiding from him, which was right. I was. But there was no way I was going to come out to say it because it would sound just too crazy. He left me his card and said if I wanted to talk, to give him a call. As I think back to that day, I wish I had called him. Maybe there would have been someone who I would be able to talk to about all of this. They all left with smiling faces as if I had calmed them down from the crazy thoughts that they might have had for me before they came up to my door.

A few days later, they ended up finding out that Officer Gliniewicz committed suicide. He made it look like a homicide so his wife could collect the insurance money. He ended up being a dirty cop with a string of embezzlement charges and inappropriate behavior that was front and center on the news for weeks. At the time, probably with all the protesting around the country about cops being bad, it was a big embarrassment for the police community.

Everything that was going on at the time was in some sort of cosmic loop that seemed to be a lot more fake than real. It did seem like it was talking to me. For instance, that big asteroid that almost hit us around Halloween at that time. You know it went in between the moon and the earth that year, and it looked just like a carved pumpkin. Or more like a human skull. To me it meant how close we had come that year to a global reset. It was so close to a year of death to a lot of the population, and I'm not talking about death from the comet either. I don't know who or what, but it's coming again. It's going to make the COVID pandemic look like a holiday. That is one of the biggest reasons I must bring this story to light. I should have come out with this story back in November of 2019, like I said I would. Maybe the whole George Floyd and COVID pandemic may never have happened. No regrets. It probably would have made it worse.

It was just one crazy thing after another. On my birthday, a year after, the Cubs won the World Series. They hadn't won in over a hundred years and it just so happened they won it on my birthday a few months after I got out. It was cool to watch everyone yelling and celebrating in front of that camera. I was watching, and it felt as if the cosmic force was telling me, "Thank you" as I was watching all the people celebrating in the streets. I was thinking, *What the hell did I go through a year ago?* And I was wondering, How many of those people are still alive because of me? Stop it, Sam! Stop it!

My wife thought I was going nuts with all the crying I was doing. I would tell her they were happy tears because of the Cubs winning the World Series and all. I tried my hardest to keep it all from her. I had to. Well, what was I supposed to say? "Oh yeah, by the way, I might be the Antichrist and that I might have saved this country from going into some kind of civil war," which still to this day I'm trying to talk myself out of.

Maybe it was all in my head, and it never happened. It was all just some crazy coincidence that my mind manifested to justify from not frying like bacon for those people down there. I tried to tell myself that somebody somewhere would have said something to me by now. There would be some sort of theologian or somebody from the press knocking on my door, but no one came, which led me to think maybe I should have written this as a fiction book. Maybe it would have made more sense.

I don't have much, if any, Internet presence. It gives me a dark feeling in the pit of my gut, so I stay away from the Internet. It's not like I would be able to talk to someone about any of this even if I wanted to.

Come to think of it, I was on a website in 2008. I was on this web page for artists where I was trying to sell my paintings online. I wasn't very successful, but it did give me an opportunity to talk to other artists. It got old after a while, just complimenting other artists the whole time. "Do you like my work?" I would ask. "Oh, I really like your work. Can I be a fan of your work?"

"Yes, of course, you will be a fan of my work," they would say."

"For sure," I would say.

"Thank you." No thank you. That got old after a while, so after like eight hundred fans, I kind of gave up on it thinking that there was no way to make any money on this thing. Maybe I wasn't as good an artist as I thought I was.

But anyway, I got back on that site after not looking at it for a few years, and it was still there. Funny, it still had a picture of me looking away from the camera, holding a newborn baby girl. My niece at the time, all wrapped up in a blanket. It was just creepy, what with everything I went through. It's almost as if it was representing new life or something.

Now I posted this way back in 2009, but it had a caption underneath it. It read, "I believe art is the oldest form of communication we have. It breaks down all barriers of language and speaks to you without having to say a word." I looked back at what I wrote back in my twenties, and it never made more sense than it does right now.

I shook my head as I was reading it. The paintings and murals that I painted back then seemed to have little clues with a special meaning behind each one of them, knowing what I know now. Like the three baby goats' picture, which had a wooden fence that stood behind them. There was one baby goat that looked as if it was up to something bad as he was ready to pounce on his baby brother. There was a painting of a wicked-looking butterfly, which looked like an angel or something too. Or there was a painting of a swan as it swam by a feeder that had three rocks in a creek bed. There was something big about the number three I still don't understand it. It was and still is a feeling I get every time I look at that number.

The site is called imagekind.com. You can still look me up, I believe. You can see it for yourself. It was almost as if I was doing some prophesying on that site, like sending a message to my future self. It was kind of cool to see it again after all these years.

My parole was over. I had about enough of this crazy TV, I was thinking. I wanted it to stop. No more Joe Gliniewicz. No more "Bungas's Normal Day." I just wanted to get back to normal. I thought that with everyone watching C-SPAN and all these other lines of communication open in this country, it was going to start changing for the better fast. Wishful thinking, right? I was trying to make things better for this country. Now I'm wishing for the days when we would all be watching Hollywood celebs and who broke up with who. I miss that. This political war in this country must stop.

Race riot after race riot. It seemed like the cops were being caught on camera doing something bad to some black guy every week. I felt bad because they never show the moments that led up to that event right away. They always let the public assume the worst first. Well, hell, anything for ratings, right? After what they always called peaceful protest was over, so was half the town. Funny, the truth of the situation always came out after all the riots and damage was already done. What do they say? A lie travels around the world three times before the truth comes to the surface.

If the media wanted this war to happen, it did seem to backfire on them. Maybe that was their plan all along, to get us to fight so the people in charge wouldn't have to fix anything and never have to own up to their mistakes. Now with their mistakes being front and center, they're not able to get away with anything anymore. It does seem the democrats hate this country by the way they talk. It's sad they never used to be that way.

There were still some weird coincidences that year, but at least they weren't directed at me. For instance, Anthony Weiner got in trouble for showing his wiener. It was like what I said about the names of the people who were closely tied to what they were doing in real life. He sent pictures of his member to an underage girl on the Internet twice. I found that kind of funny. Gross but funny.

It seemed like everyone that year was higher up on the corporate ladder, and the political scale was getting busted for something. I thought, *Good.* The Me Too movement got a little out of control. That always seems to be the case. When you don't talk about a problem long enough, the problem seems to get blown up and talked about so much that you lose sight of the problem and just start taking things too far. It almost seems people are too scared to even say hello to one another anymore. How sad.

Should I even get into Trump? Sure, why not? He was our trump card, in my opinion. I don't know why he was painted as a racist. He was in the spotlight almost his whole life; he was never called a racist before. A womanizer maybe but not a fascist or racist. We took this country back, if only for a little while, from these elites who have been running the ground for so long. Trump, I felt, spoke for the people. With not a lot of corporate donors and big money behind him, he still ended up beating Hillary Clinton.

Thank God. Some people you can just tell that they're bad people, and she was one of them. No matter what they say, they always seem like they're lying to you. You could see her discontent for Americans in her eyes.

The only reason I believe the democrats are still in office is that they promise to give poor people free stuff, which they do. So I could see if you're getting a free apartment, free food, free phone, well, I guess you should keep them elected; otherwise, those evil racist republicans will take it all away. Idiots, it's such bullshit. I guess if you're one of those people who rely on federal assistance, and if you're watching CNN all the time, I could see how you might think so. Maybe we would be able to afford all those things without the government's help if everyone would just carry their own weight, and in turn, everyone would pay less taxes and work a hell of a lot less. It would be nice to see those 1 percent gets everyone pay up to $25 per hour without raising the rates of their products. That's what I would like to see.

If you're working a construction job like me, trying to compete against someone who gets all that free stuff, it makes it nearly impossible to compete. The only way to make a living is if you get everything paid for like they do. Now I'm not racist. I do think the policies we have in place are.

Come to think of it, though. If Canada was going to pay me three times as much as what I'm making now, and their government was going to pay for my housing, food, and in some cases even my phone, then I could still speak my own language and send money back to my family on top of all that, and I didn't even have to become a Canadian citizen to do it, well, sign me up "A."

As time went on, all the race riots were still going on. I still couldn't help thinking if I had a role to play in all of this. So eventually, I got brave enough to tell my story to Tammy. I told her everything. The fact that the prison system was trying to get me to fry like bacon to get out of prison early and the whole story about the dead girl who was found in her prison cell with three types of DNA in her, and the fact that there was an officer who committed suicide over it.

Then I went on about how I laid out a plan for revenge for that girl, how I wrote a letter saying that the officer may have had something to do with it, and when they sent me back to the other prison while the Ferguson riot was about to happen.

I didn't get into the whole "Bungas's Normal Day" book that I wrote as a kid. Or how the movies that were coming out at the time might have come from a supernatural source that was pushing me to come out with this story. I think I'm crazy to this day, typing it down now.

Tammy sat back in her chair and looked at me like I was nuts, then she took a while to say something. After about ten seconds, she gave me a stern look and said to me, "Sounds like you had a hard time down there." How could that be if she had not heard anything on the news about any of this.

"It was a cover up," I said to her.

She started to do some fact-checking on her computer but didn't come up with anything I was talking about. She did find something about Officer Holt, but it didn't mention anything about his suicide letter. She kind of shrugged her shoulders and said, "Sounds like you had a hard time down there."

I felt I needed some kind of confirmation of the events that happened to me face-to-face. Holding on to this story was making me crazy. I went to my mom's house. I went to her and asked her if she remembered our conversation about the Knights Templar map. I was getting kind of excited, talking a little crazy, but I could see that I was getting nowhere by the expression on her face. Then she added maybe I should see a psychologist. When I think back to those days, maybe I should have.

I suppose I could have gone on the Internet where I would have found someone who would have investigated my story and made it mainstream. With the lack of money I had experienced and with a baby girl who needed money for diapers, I probably should have done something like that. But I kept my mouth shut.

In my mind, that promise I made about the five years of silence crossed my mind. Maybe hindsight truly is twenty-twenty, and I should just wait. If I came out with this story back then, it might have caused a ripple effect where there could have been something bad, and it would have been my fault over me needing some sort of validation or money.

I shut up and didn't talk about it to anyone else for fear of people looking at me like I was crazy. But I started to realize the longer I put off talking about it, the crazier I got, specially being sober and all. I've been clean for a while now, but when your reality doesn't match up with everyone else's reality, the mind kind of slips from man.

I couldn't' take it anymore. I didn't care about the stupid driver's license. I didn't care about cosmic pushes or beats. I was going to get myself back on the road again, and I was going to get back to work. I needed to start making money. I felt bad for Tammy working all the time. I needed to get my mind and body busy again, and I needed to start to man up and start making money. I had a little daughter to take care of, and there was nothing besides getting pulled over again that was going to stop me from living my life and supporting her. I got to spend the two years that I was on parole raising my daughter from home, and I appreciated it, but now it was my turn. I happily went back to work.

As soon as I got back to work, I got back to drinking. That's what I do, I'm sorry. The stress and soreness of working hard and drinking, for me, I guess go hand in hand. I went to work every day. My brain sometimes just needed to reboot. I cut down to once a week. With everything I went through, you would think I would have stayed away from it altogether. I guess if I had one of those jobs where I just sit there and talk to people about their problems like other people do, maybe I could stay sober. On second thought, probably not.

It's crazy, though. I don't have a problem with my alcohol intake. I get to talk to people. It's fun. I just wish there was a way for my car to drive itself home when I was ready to leave or that people would leave other people alone.

I never made that five-year promise. I kept my mouth shut. But to keep at that level of enlightenment was nearly impossible when working a full-time job. The stresses and outside forces that affect my sanity are usually met with me doing drugs and alcohol. I wish I had enough strength to fight against doing things that are bad for me. But my toxic brain lures me in every time. There is a sense of freedom that goes along with getting drunk with a group of friends or even a group of strangers. With the lack of freedom that gets shoved down our throats every year, there must be a balance somewhere.

The Ferguson Effect happened a long time ago, and maybe it will hopefully be okay to talk about this now. What truly happened to me back then in 2014, I guess I will never know for sure until someone out there will corroborate my story. People are still sensitive about all this. Since then, they have stopped militarizing cops and started to train them differently, which seems to be working. Some people still see a black person who gets accidently killed by the police or by a white person as a race thing instead of an act of defense. I still think cops' overall biggest concern is to make it home safe to their families. Sometimes I'm sure race plays a part in their split-second decisions. But if you look at the stats, they overreact and kill white people when they act aggressive too.

We never fought that civil war, but we came close. I'm kind of hoping that it won't come to that. I believe I had scared some of those elites. But most likely, what I see today is I made them angry. I believe Obama and his people are still running the show now with CNN in their corner. Their mission is and always will be to dismantle this country and the world that we're living in. When they get us to fight each other is when they can rebuild it into an America that is unrecognizable from the one you see today. Sorry, you're not supposed to say America anymore; it's United States. All of this must stop. We should be proud to be who we are. This country has done some bad things in the past, but the good outweighs the bad.

This could be coming from the Chinese too. That would make more sense. Come to think of it. If you wanted to win a war that you didn't want to fight, how would you play it? Get the people addicted to painkillers. Ban those painkillers. Then send in the fentanyl and hollow them out from the inside out with diversity training and wokeism. It's a war, but I don't know if we can fight our way out of this one. We need to pay attention. We're losing this war and losing our minds in the process. I like Trump, but if it's not going to be Trump, I know we will need somebody a lot stronger than Biden to implement the policies in this country to turn this world around before it's too late. As for me, I'm not sure if I should be celebrated or not. I'm kind of hoping this is just all part of our never-ending story.

XOXO, Sam.

ABOUT THE AUTHOR

Samuel Cole is just a man who is searching for peace and sanity in an insane world. He is always showing his love without expecting anything in return. He is funny and maybe a little crazy. He always tries to imagine what life would be like walking in someone else's shoes.

www.ingramcontent.com/pod-product-compliance
Lightning Source LLC
Chambersburg PA
CBHW022016150726
47990CB00002B/674